Arts and Crafts for the Elderly

A Resource Book for Activity Directors in Healthcare Facilities

Evelyn Lowman received her Bachelor of Arts Degree from Mary-Hardin Baylor University in Belton, Texas with majors in Speech Arts, Art, and History. She taught speech and drama in high school for a number of years and has taught private art classes wherever she has lived. Over the years she has worked as a volunteer with the elderly through church programs and health care center activities, spending the last nine years as a volunteer at Floresville Nursing Center in Floresville, Texas. There she helped the Activities Director set up a successful Arts & Crafts program and designed and executed the monthly calendars and bulletin boards, learning first hand how to adapt these programs to the elderly and the handicapped. This book is the result of that study and understanding.

Arts and Crafts
for
the Elderly

A Resource Book
for
Activity Directors
in
Healthcare Facilities

Evelyn Lowman

Springer Publishing Company
New York

Springer Publishing Company, Inc.
536 Broadway
New York, NY 10012-3955

92 93 94 95 96 / 5 4 3 2 1

Library of Congress Cataloging-in-Publication Data

Lowman, Evelyn.
    Arts and crafts for the elderly : a resource book for activity
directors in healthcare facilities / Evelyn Lowman.
      p.   cm.
    Includes bibliographical references and index.
    ISBN 0-8261-7860-X
    1. Recreational therapy for the aged. 2. Occupational therapy for
the aged. 3. Handicraft—Therapeutic use. I. Title.
RC953.8.R43L68   1992
362.1'9897—dc20   91-24182
                                        CIP

Printed in the United States of America

No matter how old you get, if you can keep the desire to be creative, you're keeping the man-child alive.

John Cassavetes

This book is dedicated
to my mother,
who taught me to laugh and love

Contents

Preface

Since the beginning of time, people have been interested in improving their environment. Early art depicted the everyday events of life by simply using the materials near at hand—clay, plants, teeth, bones, feathers, shells, skins, and furs. Later, people used works of art to enhance their rituals and worship. Handsome art objects were created to immortalize the dead, to decorate the human body, and to beautify living spaces.

Still later, many forms of art and crafts became means of fulfillment and well-being, of expressing thoughts and feelings about the world. Imagination is unique to human beings; it is what separates us from the rest of creation and it is an important part of all human development.

Many people as they grow older, lose the opportunity for creative expression—one of the greatest losses they sustain. Self-expression, making something that is uniquely one's own, has great therapeutic value for the aging, helping them to retain a measure of skill and a sense of accomplishment from improving their own environment.

Arts and Crafts for the Elderly provides help for Activity Directors in improving the quality of life in nursing homes or day care centers. A successful activity program will provide opportunities for seniors to interact socially, to build self-confidence and self-esteem, and to add satisfaction and interest in life. Carefully planned craft activities can be a great deal more than mere busywork for participants. A creative program will help residents make their center a more attractive, warm, and friendly place both for themselves and for visitors. Creative leisure time can change a seniors' attitudes toward themselves, other elderly, and the staff.

1

Key Elements for a Successful Arts and Crafts Program

PLANNING THE CRAFT PROGRAM

Activity directors of healthcare facilities often find that they never have enough time or budget to provide all the activities they would like for the residents of the home or center. *Arts and Crafts for the Elderly* addresses this need by presenting simple crafts that do not take extensive supervision, using craft materials that are inexpensive or donated. The remaining keys to a successful craft program are advanced planning and wise use of volunteers. Volunteers who have enthusiasm and a sense of humor, who are willing to plan ahead carefully for the activity sessions, and who have a caring attitude and are generous with smiles and hugs, can mean the difference between a program's success or failure. The *ideal* plan is to have once-a-month meetings of the volunteers participating in the craft program to plan the projects and the bulletin boards for the coming month. Copies of the materials and directions for the chosen project might be handed to the volunteers so they will be thoroughly familiar with the procedure. Each suggested project in *Arts and Crafts for the Elderly* has a recommended skill level, a complete materials list, fully explained steps that are numbered and given in sequence, variations that may be substituted, ideas for use or display, designs and patterns, where needed, and an explanation of therapeutic value.

BENEFITS OF A CRAFT PROGRAM

All persons, young or old, need to have their minds and souls fed. They also need to have something to look forward to that provides enjoyable work and stimulates them to use all available mental and physical resources so they will not lose their abilities.

The enormous benefits of an adequate craft program will become quite obvious after a few months. Socialization, the need to become more aware of others and the contributions each makes to the enjoyment of life, is perhaps the most important benefit. Many of the elderly seem to withdraw from contact with their associates in the home—sometimes even from friends and relatives; they simply lose interest in life. In a craft program, the use of all necessary muscles, as well as intellect, can be a big plus. Hands, arms, and mind in particular, need to be used. This use often stimulates creativity. It is surprising how many participants voice an opinion about what color or material they wish to use on *their* creation and how much better it is than someone else's choice. This helps people retain their own individuality—something many residents lose in a nursing facility. People have a much greater feeling of self-worth when they realize that they can contribute

1

to the beauty of their own rooms, to the facility which has become their home, and to those who visit the home. Everyone likes to feel capable of making a contribution to the whole. The craft program is a valuable help in relieving boredom by giving residents something to look forward to during the craft sessions. Although the majority of projects may be simple, the activity director and volunteers need to be available because most seniors will not respond to working alone: they need the stimulus of the group.

PROVIDING MOTIVATION FOR PARTICIPATION

Often seniors will be reluctant to participate in the craft activities, because they fear that their dexterity is too impaired for good results or because they have lost their desire to venture and make decisions. Motivation becomes an important element in the program. The hesitant person may be invited to watch for a while, perhaps in a small group, until he or she becomes more aware of what is being done. After the person has watched for a time, you might ask for his or her help and if he or she likes and trusts you, you are likely to get a response. Ask: "Could you cut these ribbons for us? You could help so much if you would cut out these leaf shapes. Maybe you would like to put the potpourri in these little sachets. It would really be a help if you would stuff the cotton in these little pillows." Simple requests at first are best for creating interest. Often they will become a part of the group without realizing it.

Involving the elderly in the planning of the project, using some of their ideas, is also important. Remember that projects do not have to be perfect; the experience of creating art that is one's own is the most important outcome. Sometimes people can become involved by questioning them about the crafts they enjoyed in their earlier years. They love talking about the past and you can ask: "Did you knit, crochet, quilt, sew, embroider, make dolls or doll clothes, or doll houses?" Then find a simple way to utilize that skill. Even if the skill is impaired and the person can't fully accomplish it, there will be a similar craft you can suggest. For example, those who sewed can make the simple potpourri bag by *gluing* the edges, if they are not able to use a needle or if it is dangerous for them to use a sharp instrument.

Another way to motivate is to give honest praise and appreciation for people's efforts. Make them feel their contributions are of value to the whole. Sometimes the encouragement of a friend who is participating in the program will be extremely helpful, and often the desire to give a special gift to some dear one will stimulate participation. One lady started working with crafts because she was determined to make a Christmas gift for her favorite granddaughter—that was the stimulus she needed.

Residents' wishes about joining the craft group need to be respected, especially when some continue to be reluctant. A number of these people may be reached if we know them well enough to know their fears and if we have established a feeling of trust with them. Fear is probably their greatest enemy. They may have fears that their handicaps will make them seem inadequate in the eyes of others. Fear of missing a meal (probably the most important event of their day) or fear of missing their medication may also be prevalent fears. These fears should be dealt with by assuring them that they will be through in time for lunch or dinner, that they will receive medications on time, and by always keeping one's word. Some incontinent elderly may be afraid of being away from an available bathroom. If there is a problem in this area, be sure someone is alerted to attend to their needs in an unobtrusive way.

Many elderly suffer from depression; these people are the hardest to motivate. Sometimes we must admit defeat and quietly try to include them in the activities as much as possible. Some seniors will be able to make gifts or craft items for craft fairs or art shows and these accomplishments can add a sense of excitement and achievement if projects are carefully planned and carried out. Many of the best craft efforts may be used as prizes for bingo, especially well-made jewelry, small decorated containers for cards, soaps, or jewelry and handkerchiefs. Potpourri bags and small decorative stuffed pillows also make lovely prizes. Residents of nursing centers should be encouraged to use their craft work in their rooms for decorative or storage purposes and to add a unique personal touch to their home place.

Sharing is extremely important in adding quality to life and in providing motivation. Seniors like to make greeting cards for family or for friends in the hospital and enjoy making gifts for members of their families or their companions in the home. At Easter, one nursing center makes numerous small Easter baskets and decorates eggs for the baskets. Then they invite children from a day care center for an Easter egg hunt and everyone enjoys the occasion—especially the hosts.

Community organizations provide numerous Christmas parties and gifts for residents of nursing homes, yet the elders want to feel that they have something important to give others. This can certainly be a motivating factor. Craft sessions for the few months preceding Christmas can be directed to making gifts for needy or other community children's groups, with a party planned for presenting the gifts. This can become a yearly activity for the center.

If the facility has a yearly open house for the community (most nursing centers do) the seniors can make flowers or table decorations to suit the particular theme of the occasion. It builds confidence to feel you can contribute to a party in your home. There are many ideas in this book for such activities.

Men seem harder to motivate than women, probably because their work did not usually include any arts and crafts; so they see such activities as women's work. Some men will enjoy working with wood projects because they are more familiar with hammers, nails, and sandpaper. Since sharp tools should not be used in a nursing facility, previously cut patterns may be ordered for such projects as bird houses and bird feeders and for wooden toys. The bird houses and feeders can be enjoyed by all the residents of the home; putting out feed for birds is an excellent way to make the elderly feel needed, responsible, and at home. The wooden toys can be sanded and glued together to give as gifts at the Christmas party, especially to those children who might not otherwise have a Christmas gift.

Men should be encouraged to sand and finish the cut plywood or chipboard pieces used as supports for plaques, trivets, or the tick-tack-toe game. Working with clay is therapeutic for both men and women and they enjoy it if the projects are suited to their skills and interests, because clay is an active, physical activity. They may also be interested in making dominoes or wind chimes.

Many nursing centers regularly take photographs of seniors on special occasions. Pictures can be taken of them working at their craft sessions, and the slides shown later on the movie screen. People love seeing themselves and find their craft work more interesting when seen in picture form. All of these suggestions are directed at motivation of the elderly to participate.

SKILL LEVELS

It is difficult to find suitable crafts for use with the elderly who have varying levels of skill. In *Arts and Crafts for the Elderly*, the level of skill needed for each project is indicated by code in the upper right corner of the page. There is also a chart that recommends which projects to use with each skill level. Limitations associated with such conditions as stroke, arthritis, poor eyesight, mental impairment, and short attention span must always be considered.

Elderly who have use of only one hand can work with another more skilled person. A person with one hand can hold the paper in place while another paints or punches a design. They can put potpourri in a bag or stuffing in a pillow. The one-handed person can hold the ends of yarn tightly while someone else braids the yarn or they can dip paper strips in papier-mâché paste. One hand can even do weaving with a large plastic shuttle or needle after the loom is warped. By looking carefully through the projects, you will find numerous places where persons with one hand can be of use while working with others. For those whose eyesight is poor, be sure to use light colors, as dark-colored materials are hard to see. **Most** *of the elderly need light colors to work with.* People with vision problems can also dip papier-mâché strips, knead clay, cut lengths of ribbon if given a pattern, fill bags with potpourri, wind yarn on cardboard for others to use, and accomplish other simple tasks to help the more skilled. This kind of cooperation is in itself a valuable social activity.

Often less able residents like to cut with scissors and can do it very well. They can cut out the shapes for the monthly calendars or for other decorations, cut paper strips for papier-mâché work, cut quilt pieces from wallpaper, if the shapes are drawn on the back of the paper, and they can cut crepe paper strips for flowers. There are many projects in this book which require cutting with scissors; if this is what some participants like to do best, let them do most of the cutting work. If they are not capable of using sharp scissors, provide safety scissors.

Those who have enjoyed sewing in the past like pulling threads for the edges of napkins or other fabric projects; and, as long as the fabric is a light color, they never seem to tire of the job.

There may be a few women who have their sewing machines. If so, let them sew up simple seams for potpourri bags or quilt squares. Almost all of the less skilled can do glue work if they are checked by volunteers and helped with the placement of materials. Many of them like to dip and dye eggs for the Easter baskets while the more skilled do the decorating and finishing. All of the less skilled can knead clay; this is a good activity for everyone. The whole craft program needs to become a *cooperative effort* with the skilled, less skilled and handicapped contributing where they are able.

IMPORTANCE OF BULLETIN BOARDS AND ACTIVITY CALENDARS FOR REALITY ORIENTATION

One of the most important sections in *Arts and Crafts for the Elderly* is Part VIII, which contains ideas for bulletin boards. Bulletin boards are very necessary in the life of the center because they enable seniors to relate to the days, months, and seasons of the year, to stay alert to the life and activities of the community of which they are a part, and to help keep their happy memories alive. Fresh ideas for interesting and colorful bulletin boards along with the necessary activity calendars are included in abundance—several ideas for each month in the year, all with patterns.

Most individuals enjoy seeing pictures of themselves displayed in various ways. In Part VIII, the drawings of the little train, the cars, and houses along the street are good examples of bulletin board designs just right for putting faces in the windows. Photos on Christmas tree ornaments for a nursing home family tree are enjoyed by both residents and their families. It is important to remember that the elderly like familiar things, children, animals and birds, talking about things that happened long ago, old time music and songs, and remembering all the special times of their lives.

The most important aspects of any craft program in nursing homes or day care centers are designed to help seniors feel useful and needed, to relieve boredom, to aid in social interaction, to bring back happy memories, to help retain dignity and individuality, to foster feelings of accomplishment, and to improve the home environment. The right program can truly make life more enjoyable—so, **have fun!**

MATERIALS FOR A BASIC CRAFT PROGRAM

One of the great needs an activity director has in a long-term care facility is money to budget the program. Therefore, this book suggests as many projects as possible using inexpensive, easy-to-find, or donated materials.

The basic materials needed are clays, a variety of papers and glues, paints, and the various tools needed for working with these materials. All other necessary items will be indicated with the particular project.

POTENTIAL HAZARDS OF MATERIALS

Activity directors and volunteers need to be aware of the hazards involved in using certain materials with elderly who may suffer various degrees of dementia. The recipe given for papier-mâché paste is safe to use and will not irritate the skin, and the Ross paste suggested is nontoxic and easy to keep without refrigeration. Spray paint or clear acrylic spray should not be used by the seniors and should only be used out-of-doors by the director or volunteers. Some elderly can use any scissors safely, but some must be given safety scissors to use. Only table knives should be used by the seniors; all cutting with sharp craft knives can be done ahead of time by the director or volunteers. Candles are not lighted in nursing homes, but candle holders can still be used without lighting the candles. Pins and needles are to be used with special care—only those who are capable and in full control of faculties should be allowed to use them. Others may use toothpicks for punching. Disposable plastic gloves are available from paint stores or from craft supply companies for those who have very sensitive skin. Acrylic and tempera paint are nontoxic, but seniors must be watched so they do not put paints in their mouths. White glue, tacky glue, and rainbow glue are nontoxic, but spray glue, Duco glue, and some fabric glues can be toxic and should be used only in an outdoor setting. *Read labels carefully before using any product with the elderly.* If some material being used in the craft session looks good enough to eat, be careful—someone will take a bite.

TOOLS FOR ENLARGING PATTERNS

If the center owns an opaque projector, quick and easy enlargement or reduction of patterns or pictures is possible. There is an inexpensive projector on the market for artists (See appendix). Because most centers have limited budgets, a simple wooden or metal pantograph, costing from twelve to twenty dollars is a good investment. Be sure to buy one with instructions for its use and *save* the instruction sheet. The pantograph is made with wooden bars, marked accurately for enlarging or reducing from twelve to thirty ratios. The smaller 13 inch pantograph that enlarges up to twelve ratios should be adequate for all your needs. These instruments are great timesavers. By using a pantograph, pictures in books and magazines can easily be enlarged for use. When enlarging from this book, trace the pattern on a sheet of bond paper and enlarge from the tracing. Be sure to tape down the small tracing and the paper on which you will trace the enlargement, *so they will not move* during the drawing.

MATERIALS SAVED OR DONATED

Many other supplies necessary for the program will be inexpensive scrap items that can be saved and donated by interested individuals or groups in the community. Specific lists of needed articles should be provided to friends of the center to avoid donation of materials that cannot be used. Many businesses in the community will gladly save discards if asked. Local gift shops may save scrap materials such as ribbons, papers, small boxes; wallpaper outlets may contribute books of discontinued wallpaper patterns; and interior designers will donate fabric samples. Picture frame shops may donate matboard scraps for making small individual looms and mounts for artwork.

Be sure to pick up donated materials on a regular basis so contributors will be encouraged to continue their help.

The following is a list of materials friends in the community can donate. You will add others to your own list.

Laces	Yarns	Christmas and seasonal cards
Trims	Fabric scraps	Food containers
Ribbons	Felt pieces	Small cardboard or plastic boxes
Sequins	Cords of all kinds	Foil from gift plants
Buttons	Leather strips	Gift wrappings
Glitter	Artificial flowers	Wood scraps
Natural materials	Brown paper bags	Strawberry baskets

Old hats for an Easter fashion show
Old sheets for making tablecloths and for painting murals
Magazines with beautiful pictures, including colorful seed catalogues

List *only* the items you want and can use.

IDEAS FOR STORAGE OF MATERIALS

Organized storage is a great asset to activity directors of nursing homes or other facilities. The following storage ideas are offered as suggestions.

Open shelf storage provides the most accessible method of storing necessary materials. Everything can be seen at a glance if the contents of storage containers are carefully marked. Cardboard boxes with strong lids, at least five to six inches deep and all the same size, make the best containers for storage and can be stacked two to a shelf. Many times the kitchen of the nursing facility can provide such boxes, or various businesses in the community might be able to save matching boxes for the center. Boxes should be marked clearly on the ends with a heavy black marker, labeling the contents.

Old kitchen serving trays, painted in various colors make fine individual work trays for each resident. Names put on trays with masking tape make for easy removal when residents leave. The tray contains the necessary items used in crafting: water container, paint container, small flat dish for glue, brushes or other tools. Small muffin tins for each tray make wonderful containers for holding sequins, glitter, buttons, pasta, and small shells for use on projects and can also be used to hold paint or glue. All trays should have a sponge or wet towels for cleaning the hands.

Any plastic container can hold water; plastic lids from coffee cans, or other flat plastic lids can be used for glue or papier-maché paste.

Various other available boxes may be utilized for storage: shoe boxes, gift cartons, and large cans are good for storing smaller items such as shells, pasta, sequins, pebbles, etc.

Paint the names of contents on the side of containers in large letters to be easily seen. Larger, more bulky materials should be stored in the largest boxes along with all the tools and equipment needed for the craft sessions.

Some shelves should be saved for large, heavy items, wallpaper sample books, collected materials and containers, spray paints and other paints, glues and all varieties of paper. The tops of shelves should be saved as space for drying clay and papier mache articles.

A large box with labeled dividers could be used for patterns, cards, paper sacks, matboard or cardboard, and any flat materials, including large manilla envelopes. The envelopes are excellent for storing collections of pictures and for craft decorating ideas from magazines and other sources. Each envelope should correspond to—and supplement—each part of the book. The envelopes should be labeled "Part I," "Part II," etc. so you always know which section of the book is being enriched.

At the end of each part of the book there is a blank page for notes. You might add any ideas or changes that occur to you as the projects are used: a change in the materials or the order of the steps in the procedure, to notes about other creative ways to use the suggested activity, or any adverse reactions of the residents that would necessitate a change in methods. To better adapt the activities to your own group, make your notations clearly and record page numbers for reference.

THE VALUE OF CRAFT FAIRS, ART COMPETITIONS, ART SHOWS

Late fall is an ideal time to plan a craft fair if your facility can produce quality items. An undertaking of this kind involves a great deal of work and planning, but provides enormous excitement for the seniors. If a fair is planned, baked goods provided by community friends and volunteers can be added to the salable items, and games, music, and perhaps some other entertainment could be provided for the enjoyment of the elderly and guests. There are groups and individuals in almost any community who will gladly contribute time and talent to this project. Posters might be made for advertising, placed in strategic locations around the community. A special theme could be used, such as a circus theme with clowns and lots of balloons. Any money made should go toward replenishing the craft program.

Art Competitions

An art competition can add excitement to the life of the nursing center and it is not necessary to have fine works of art for this endeavor. Look through the book for the ideas suggested for such a program. They are scattered throughout the book and their suitability is indicated at the end of the project under "Use" or "Display." Some entries might be group projects. If there are various wings in the nursing center, they might compete by wings. In this case, some larger painting could be executed such as group painting on a sheet or tablecloth painted in a design the participants create themselves. If a competition is planned and carried out, first, second, and third place ribbons should be presented to the participants and work should be judged by an impartial group of people from the community. Be sure that everyone entering receives something for his entry, whether it be a ribbon, a small gift, or a flower.

Divisions might include murals, individual paintings, batiks, tie-dye, ceramics, quilts, and any other categories, depending on crafts used in the facility.

Serve a buffet luncheon so residents can choose from the foods prepared: salads, sandwiches, fresh fruits, cheeses, hors d'oeuvres, drinks, and several desserts. This is an opportunity for them to decide what appeals to them.

Art Shows

If it is not feasible for your facility to have a craft fair or an art competition, try having an art show. Display the work of the seniors, trying to use at least one item from each member of the craft group. Invite friends of the nursing home in the community and families of the residents. Make it a festive occasion and serve refreshments. The craft classes can make a tablecloth and flowers for the serving table. This creates interest in the craft program and builds self-esteem in the elderly.

SIMPLE ART LESSONS FOR THE AGING

Collage is an art form that is a natural for use with the aging. The materials needed can be found almost anywhere. Use dark heavy paper or matboard scraps as mounts or bases for the designs, tacky glue for holding the collage, and objects such as paper clips, old keys, looseleaf notebook reinforcements, toothpicks, pressed leaves, tiny shells, or buttons for mounting. All kinds of papers—construction, art, tissue, foil, wallpaper, textured papers, wrapping paper—and any other available materials can be used. Fabrics can also be used to make interesting collages.

A number of simple outline designs can be made available to the participants, or they may simply make up their own design, cutting or tearing paper and incorporating other items to make a pleasing arrangement. A volunteer should work out a simple collage as a demonstration and help the seniors organize their own ideas in order to design their collage. Give each person a piece of mounting board, some glue, their choice of objects for mounting and encourage him or her to lay the design out on the mount *before* gluing down. Any design produced is acceptable. Art materials are not sacred: Art should be produced for the joy of self-expression.

Acrylic or watercolor painting can be a memorable and enjoyable experience for the elderly if they are motivated and encouraged to venture and experiment. The materials needed are:

Jar acrylics or watercolors;
Brushes;
A 9×12 block of 90 lb. watercolor paper (a block usually contains 25 sheets);
Containers for water;
Plastic lids or other discarded flat white lids for mixing paint;
Sponge for wetting paper;
Items for producing texture—small spray bottle with water, a bit of rubbing alcohol with a dropper, cut-out stencils, stamping tools (round caps or corks, edge of matboard), salt, plastic wrap or wax paper, old toothbrush for spatter, pieces of heavy string, nonwaterproof marking pens, wax crayons, white glue;
Paper towels and plenty of water for cleaning up.

There are a number of ways to use the materials, depending on the skill and interest level of the seniors. For those who are interested, there could be an art lesson once or twice a week. The more skilled can learn to paint simple pictures. Most communities will have an artist who can be approached to give several hours a week as a volunteer to teach the elderly. The artist leader should demonstrate on an easel located so all can see and follow each step.

The following procedure (or any procedure desired by the artist) might be used.

1. As a first picture, draw a simple landscape on watercolor paper. (See 1-1). Draw sky, a row of mountains, a tree line, a lake or road with a few closer trees in very uncomplicated forms—just shapes. Use only two or three colors and paint with simple washes and a bit of shading with a darker mix of the same two colors, such as blue and burnt sienna. The background colors will be lighter (farther away) and the foreground colors darker (closer). It might be more interesting if the class suggests the scene, if the demonstrating artist is willing. Ask: "Do you want mountains or trees or both? a house or a barn or a windmill? a road or a pond or stream? birds or people?"

1-1 Landscapes

2. In the second lesson, use the same landscape but add a very simple house or barn shape in the distant landscape so it will not have many details.

3. In the third lesson, add simple figures or birds, just forms, if desired. Perhaps the class will choose to leave the painting just the way it is, very uncomplicated, since they will be following the steps with their own paintings.

4. In a fourth lesson, try a sky, seashore, and sand dunes, just shapes. You might add a simple boat shape or some gulls. Always keep everything simple, particularly shapes, and use few colors, no more than three at a time. Add yellow ochre to the blue and sienna above in order to work with three primaries. Brighter colors may be added later.

In creating artwork, always try to think of the picture in terms of pleasing shapes and to create forms by placing dark colors against light and light against the darks.

Ask questions: "What are the colors we used? How does red make you feel? What do you think of when you see yellow or orange? Does blue make you feel good? Why do you think so? How do purple or black make you feel? What do you think about when you see those colors? How do you feel about green? What is your favorite color?" This can tell you something about the person's feelings. Bright cheerful colors or dark, dull, and depressing colors can be an indication of a relatively happy person or a depressed one.

After the seniors have painted several pictures and have become more confident, they might be encouraged to paint on their own with just a simple drawing sketched on their paper for them. They should be told to use any colors they like. Skies can be any color—the pinks and lavenders of dawn, the greys of a cloudy or rainy day, the golds and reds of a sunset or blues and grey whites for sunshiny days. Trees do not have to be green and mountains can be any color. Show them some examples of primitive paintings for inspiration, paintings of Grandma Moses, Tella Kitchen, or others like them. Then ask: "What do you remember about your childhood? About Christmas? What did you play, what did you do for fun, what kind of work did you or your family do? What special times do you remember: weddings, hayrides, dances, parties, quilting bees? How did the houses, stores, churches look; what was inside; were there autos and trains, or horses and wagons, or buggies? How did you dress? Paint pictures of some of the things you can see in your mind and memory.

A way to interest those who are not capable of painting their own pictures is to use simple pictures or photographs on heavy paper and let the class use acrylic paint to paint over the printed picture, then mount the painting and let them hang the work in their room. Pictures on out-of-date calendars are good for this activity as they are generally printed on rather heavy paper, but they do need to be very simple pictures, not too detailed.

Another simple way to paint is to use texturing materials.

1. Dampen a piece of watercolor paper with a sponge and put a *deep*-colored wash on the paper. Sprinkle the wet paper with a little table salt and when dry, brush it off to leave a nice starry texture or lovely flower shape. Add stems and leaves to the flower shapes and a few misty tree shapes to the landscape.

2. Squeeze a piece of plastic wrap in your hand and lay it in the *deep*-colored wet wash, weight it down with something until dry, remove to find a lovely abstract design. Waxed paper can be laid flat in a deep-colored wash to create the same effect. Then other forms can be added to the abstract background—a few flowers, a few tree shapes, rocks along the shore, or whatever you see in the design.

3. Dip a piece of heavy string in one color paint and arrange it in a design on a deeper colored background to make a lovely picture. Put the string on the wet wash and remove it before it is dry.

4. Lay a stencil on a dry colored wash and fill in the stencil with a contrasting color or lay a stencil on the paper and spatter around it; remove to find a lovely pattern. Wonderful stencils can be ordered very inexpensively from Dover Publications.

5. Stamp in a wet wash with the edge of a piece of matboard or the edge of a tongue depressor, a cork, a round cap or a small sponge to form another nice abstract.

6. Spray or drip drops of water in a deep-colored damp wash to make star-shaped designs. Those can look like a starry sky if the wash is dark enough.

7. A few drops of rubbing alcohol dripped into a dark green or blue wet wash will look like bubbles rising through the water and a fish and a bit of seaweed might be added to the picture.

8. Sprinkle tempera powder in two colors, blue and yellow or red and blue, onto a clear wet wash of water and watch the colors spread and join to make a third color.

Small lengths of lath can be put together by the men or mats can be cut from matboard scraps to make frames for the artwork. The lath or mat can be covered with glued-on fabric, if desired, or the lath can be painted or stained.

The less skilled can also enjoy creating art. In the batik section of the book, there are simple and charming art creations for the less skilled as well as those who are more capable. This special technique using white glue and wax crayons can help the less skilled to have more self-confidence. Simple doodling with colored markers on white paper is plain fun and if nonwaterproof markers are used, the finished drawings can be dampened to look lovely when the colors run together. Any activity is preferable to enforced idleness.

According to the book *Drawing on the Artist Within* (Edwards, 1988), you can interpret feelings using the doodling or lines people make. Edwards considers line drawings as subconscious thought made visible. Give the seniors a piece of white paper and a pencil or pen and ask them to draw lines on their paper, just lines, wherever they want them. If they make sharp, jagged, stabbing lines, it can indicate anger; circular curving forms, usually rising, indicate joy and happiness; horizontal lines indicate peacefulness; down-turned lines or lines drawn at the bottom of the paper indicate depression. These will not hold true for everyone but it can be a very interesting observation.

The more handicapped seniors can be encouraged to produce a mural as a group project. Stretch a piece of white sheet or canvas on a 3×4-foot wood frame. Cover the fabric with white latex house paint to make a more rigid painting surface. This is easier done out-of-doors. Let the paint surface dry thoroughly. If the residents are to paint inside, place heavy plastic dropcloths under the painting surface. Give each worker small containers of complementary colors and encourage them to brush, drip, dab or pour the paint on the canvas. If the design doesn't look just right, turn it upside down or sideways and see how it looks. If it still doesn't suit, you can always cover it with another coat of latex and let them try again. Generally these "canvasses" can dry to make surprisingly nice abstract paintings. Many famous artists have done it this way.

In order to display the residents' artwork, a small bulletin board hung in each room is a good investment. Artwork displayed on bulletin boards can be changed frequently and easily. Notes and reminders can also be pinned on the room boards. Some of the artwork can be displayed on a central bulletin board, and the best work can be displayed in an art show.

KEY TO CODES FOR SKILL LEVELS

The symbol for each skill level is found in the upper right-hand corner of the first page of each project. You can tell at a glance the *primary* level of skill required.

> *Level One,* the **handicapped** symbol indicates a **very short attention span** of perhaps no more than 10 minutes and a **need for almost continuous instruction and guidance.** (See Figure 1-2.)
>
> 1-2
>
> *Level Two,* the **less able** symbol, indicates a **shorter attention span** than the able (15 to 25 minutes), need for **repeated instructions,** no fine detail or finishing work, and **frequent supervision** and guidance. (See Figure 1-3.)
>
> 1-3
>
> *Level Three,* the **very able** symbol, indicates an attention span of 30 minutes to 60 minutes, good hand-eye coordination, ability to follow directions after being shown and to perform fairly detailed work. (See Figure 1-4.)
>
> 1-4

Projects that can be used with the handicapped will have that symbol in the upper right hand corner along with the other two symbols, because levels two and three can also enjoy the more simple crafts. Some projects can be used for celebrations or holiday decorations and will be denoted by a circle with a dot (See Figure 1-5). On the following page you will find a chart indicating exactly which projects are suitable for each skill level.

1-5

Chart of Skill Levels for Various Projects

The whole craft program should be a cooperative effort with persons of varying skill levels contributing as they are able. If the handicapped are set apart from the group and given only very simple work to do, they frequently lose interest. They need the stimulus of the group. The following skill level chart has been organized to serve as a guide only. The handicapped can make some *small* contribution to nearly every project and the less skilled and the very skilled can enjoy most of the simple crafts.

PROJECTS SUITABLE FOR THE HANDICAPPED: LEVEL ONE

Part II
Handprints and poem—suitable for every senior;
Collage, for feeling—materials need to be cut ahead;
Folded paper chains—only the angel shape for this level;
Decorated paper napkins and variations;
Papier-mâché napkin rings—can glue strips for covering;
Papier-mâché candleholders—can glue strips;
Nature prints;
Finger painting;
Easter eggs—can do dipping;
Spirals—can do only if able to cut on lines;
Mobiles—can dip and glue ribbons on balloon mobile;
Waxed paper transparencies—can do if crayons are shredded ahead.

Part III
Clay, self-hardening—can knead clay, play with it, can roll coils, cut shapes with cutters;
Baker's clay—can knead, roll, cut shapes, paint with foam brush, cut shapes with cutters;
Clay key chains—can knead, roll, cut shapes, stick on decals;
Simple clay magnets—can knead, roll, cut shapes, paint with foam brush, use stick-on decals;
Simple clay jewelry—can cut in shapes with cutter, paint with foam brush.

Part IV
Drip design on paper;
Design with crayons;
Glue drawing—will need a little help with design;
Dippity-dye batik.

Part V
Whimsical yarn designs—can use the simple circle designs, grapes or circle flowers;
Fabric potpourri bags—can make net bags tied with ribbons;
Vegetable prints—will need some help with printing;
Leaf prints—will need some help with printing;
Felt Christmas stockings—can put glue line on edge of one piece of stocking and glue on some
    decorations;
Patchwork—can glue simple squares on a backing, if lines are drawn;
Feeling books—can help glue materials on pages.

Part VI
Plant, popcorn containers—can glue and wrap yarn with help to keep yarn close together;
Popcorn florals—with drawing for placement of corn;
Pencil and pen holders—can stick on stamps or decals;
Coasters for wet glasses—can stick decals on cork rounds;
Berry baskets—can cut ribbons if given a pattern;
Octopus—can hold ends for braiding, some can braid;
Pasta and shell jewelry—can string pasta with a plastic needle.

Part VII
Wreaths—can cut ribbons to right length with pattern;
Christmas placemats—can cut out simple pictures and glue on mat;
Christmas picture ornaments—can glue on their own picture;
Candy cane decorations—can slip insertion lace on canes;
Advent calendars—can cut or glue pictures if shown the proper location.

PROJECTS SUITABLE FOR THE LESS SKILLED: LEVEL TWO

Part II
Doily nosegays—can do the simple parts, such as wrapping stems;
Pierced designs;
Autumn leaves;
Folded paper chains—help with folding, draw outline with the help of a template;
Papier-mâché jewelry;
Papier-mâché candleholders;
Nature prints;
Easter eggs—can dye and glue on stickers;
Spirals—if able to cut on lines, can add hanging decorations;
Mobiles—try less difficult designs;

Part III
Self-hardening clay—knead, roll, do some pinch, coil, or slab work;
Baker's clay—can cut shapes with cutter, paint and decorate;
Clay name tags—need help with names;
Simple clay jewelry.

Part IV
Can do all batik work except tie-dye and can do parts of that, wrapping with string or rubber bands.

Part V
Simple weaving—after the loom is warped;
Whimsical yarn designs—use less complicated designs;
Writing with yarn—need help with words;
Fabric potpourri bags—can glue sides and fill with potpourri;
Vegetable prints;
Leaf prints;
Christmas stockings—can do the less difficult work, gluing sides and adding decorations;
Patchwork—try the less difficult patterns;
Feeling books—can do all of the gluing.

Part VI
Pencil and pen holders;
Coasters—can do gluing and decals;
Berry baskets—can do less difficult parts such as weaving ribbon or gluing flowers on sides;
Octopus—can braid and stuff;
Bath soaps—can do less difficult parts, gluing trims;
Pasta jewelry—can string with plastic needle;
Tic-tac-toe game—can make clay tokens.

Part VII
Wreaths;
Christmas placements;
Christmas picture ornaments—cut and glue their own pictures;
Candy cane sleigh—can do less difficult parts, glue trims;
Candy cane decoration;
Plastic foam ball decoration—can insert greenery and bows;
Advent calendars—can glue pictures on backing;
Party decorations—can help with painting on tablecloths and making flowers.

PROJECTS SUITABLE FOR THE SKILLED WORKER: LEVEL THREE

Most projects already listed will be enjoyed by the skilled worker.

Part II
Bookmarks;
Paper flowers;
Fallover eggs;
Easter eggs—finish work;
Mobiles.

Part III
All self-hardening clay construction;
All glue dough projects;
Clay jewelry—finish work.

Part IV
Tie-dye and rubbings.

Part V
Loom weaving;
Eyes of God;
Writing with yarn;
Tablecloths from old sheets;
Felt pillows—the less skilled can help;
Christmas stockings—finish work, other levels can help;
Patchwork—cutting patterns, more difficult work.

Part VI
Spice containers—less skilled can attach decals;
Coasters—finish work;
Berry baskets—finish work;
Bath soap—finish work;
Pasta Christmas trees;
Shell or pasta boxes;
Tick-tack-toe game.

Park VII
Candy cane sleigh—finish work;
Hanging ball decoration;
Advent calendars;
All party decorations.

Part VIII
The more skilled can help with many of the bulletin boards, particularly with cutting out activity
   calendar designs.

PREPARATION FOR PROJECTS

1. Cover tables with newspaper or plastic to protect table and to reduce glare for the seniors. Covering is absolutely necessary for projects using clay, glue, or paint.
2. Gather participants and seat at table.
3. Explain the project.
4. Show a finished product if possible.
5. Place all materials needed for project on tables, giving each participant a tray or flat box containing all materials necessary.
6. Let the seniors choose their colors, designs, and materials, if possible. They should be encouraged to make all the decisions they are able or willing to make.
7. If the project is coded for the handicapped or less skilled, those who are more able should be encouraged to help. *Parts* of nearly every project can be done by the less skilled.
8. Volunteers should be enthusiastic about the work session and should be throughly familiar with the project. This involves planning ahead.
9. Enlarge designs to suit your needs or spaces, using a pantograph or other enlarger.

10. Always have water and wet paper towels or other towels handy for keeping hands free of glue, clay, paint.

11. Indicate how the project will be used or displayed. It needs to have some function. It may be shown in a display case, used on the bulletin boards, in the resident's room, used to decorate the halls, to decorate the tables for parties, for birthdays or other special occasions, for gifts or art shows.

12. Involve seniors in a discussion of the project, if suitable. For example, the quilting project, ask: "When did you make your first quilt, if you made one? What was the pattern? What did you do with it?" Many of the projects can involve discussion and stimulate memories.

13. Each project should be adapted to fit the needs of the particular facility and its residents.

14. It is important to help workers clean hands and return to their rooms.

15. Many projects will be carryovers from one craft session to another because of drying time or because some are more time consuming, but workers seem to like these projects, perhaps because of familiarity with the procedure.

2

Paper Crafts and Papier-Mâché

CUT PAPER CRAFTS

NOSEGAYS FROM PAPER DOILIES

Materials

Paper doilies—two per worker, one 6-inch and one 8-inch;
Small artificial flowers, daisies, violets, roses, and baby's breath, all with stems and leaves, three
  or four for each worker;
Green floral tape;
Scissors;
Masking tape;
Soft florist's wire; and
Narrow ribbon—2 yards for each nosegay.

To Do Ahead—Director or Volunteers

Have all materials except flowers ready for each worker, let them choose the flowers they prefer. See Figure 2-1 as a guide.

2-1 Guide

16

Directions

1. Center the smaller 6-inch doily on top of the 8-inch doily and punch a tiny hole in the exact center through both doilies. Use the tip of the scirrors.
2. With masking tape, tape the stems of the flowers together and put them through the hole in the doilies.
3. Tape stems securely to the back side and wrap all stems together with green floral tape to form one stem.
4. Pull the doilies up, gather softly around the flowers and secure at the back by wrapping with soft wire (see Figure 2-2).
5. Add ribbon streamers, 10 inches long, to the stems on the back side of nosegay.
6. This makes a lacy, flower-filled nosegay for use in spring.

Variation

If you wish to use the nosegay for a birthday, attach an attractive, small name tag, printed on each side, to one of the ribbons (see Figure 2-3).

Use or Display

Use as May Day decoration beside each door or for each resident's room. Use as a birthday remembrance instead of the usual florist carnation in a vase. This would be a welcome change and the workers would enjoy making them in the craft session.

Therapeutic Value

Social value—sense of community and cooperation; eye-hand coordination;
Physical use of hands and arms—muscle stimulation;
Sense of self-worth—making something to be used for birthday parties or to use in one's room;
Reality orientation—May Day.

2-2 Wrapped Stems

2-3 Print on Opposite Sides

PIERCED DESIGNS ON WHITE PAPER

Materials

White drawing paper or other heavy white paper;
Several sizes of tapestry needles for punching;
Round toothpicks for punching;
Paper punch for larger holes;
Colored paper for mounting—construction or art paper;
White glue; and
Pieces of foam packing or heavy corrugated cardboard to lay the paper on for punching.

To Do Ahead—Director or Volunteers

Designs given here are designed for piercing, but almost any desired design can be used. Trace designs, enlarging if necessary with pantograph. By covering the back of your tracing with pencil graphite, it can be transferred to the white paper, or use copier.

Directions

1. Trace and enlarge the patterns. Have the various designs (see Figure 2-4) on the work tables and let the workers choose their designs.
2. Give each person a large tapestry needle, toothpick, or other punching tool, a piece of corrugated board or foam to lay paper on for punching. Punch from the back where the drawing is, and on all inside lines.
3. Let them punch out the design, holes about ¼ inch apart, making some different sized holes for variety. Cut around the outside of the design when finished punching.
4. Turn the punched design over to the front and mount with glue on colored paper; cut a little larger than the punched design.

Use or Display

These make wonderful decorations for a Valentine bulletin board. (See section VIII on bulletin boards). They may also be used as decorative hangings for the residents' rooms. If designs are used for the bulletin board, cut on outer lines instead of mounting. Designs are to be traced and enlarged to twice their size on a pantograph, larger if you wish.

Therapeutic Value

Ideas and creativity—choosing designs, a means of self-expression;
Physical stimulation—eye-hand coordination and muscle use;
Social value—conversation, cooperation;
Sense of self-worth—contribution to the whole, using creations on bulletin boards or in rooms.

2-4 Patterns

BOOKMARKS—PIERCED AND DRIED MATERIALS

Materials for Pierced Bookmark

Heavy white drawing or other white paper;
Fineline felt-tip pen in black or blue;
Large tapestry needles or toothpicks for punching;
Colored paper—construction or art paper;
Paper punch;
Scissors;
Narrow ribbon or cord;
Pieces of corrugated cardboard to use as a base for piercing.

To Do Ahead—Director or Volunteers

Cut heavy white paper into 2 × 7 inch pieces (depending on name to be written, be sure paper is long enough).

Directions

1. Fold the strip of cut paper down the exact center and write name on fold in slanting script, *keeping bottom of name on fold line* (see Figure 2-5).
2. Keep the paper folded and pierce through *both* sides of paper at the same time with a large tapestry needle, a toothpick, or other piercing tool.
3. Unfold and mount on colored paper with the writing on the bottom side and the pierced side up. Cut the mounting paper ¼ inch larger than the white pierced paper.
4. Punch hole at top with paper punch and loop a narrow ribbon through the hole.

Use or Display

These can be used by residents who read or given as gifts.

Therapeutic Value

Ideas and creativity—choosing materials for flower bookmark;
Physical stimulation—eye-hand coordination;
Social value—sense of community, sharing, and giving gifts;
Sense of self-worth—giving a gift to family or friends.

2-5 Guide—Pierced Bookmark

Materials for Dried Leaf or Flower Bookmark

Dried and pressed small leaves, flowers, or weeds;
Sheets of clear acetate, 9 × 12—See appendix for source;
Paper punch;
Scissors;
Narrow ribbon or colored cord;
Tacky glue;
Paper clips.

Do Ahead—Director or Volunteers

Cut the acetate into 2 × 6 or 2 × 7 inch strips, two for each worker.

Directions

1. Give each worker a few of the dried materials or let workers choose their own.
2. Have them arrange the materials in a pleasing design on one piece of the acetate. Glue down (see Figure 2-6).
3. Run a narrow solid line of glue around the borders of the bottom piece of acetate.
4. Place the top piece over, matching exactly at the edges and weight down with a book until dry, about two hours or longer.
5. Punch hole in top end and tie ribbon through hole.

Use or Display

These can be used by residents who read or given as gifts to friends.

2-6 Guide—Flower Bookmark

PRINTS ON PAPER

AUTUMN LEAVES FROM BROWN PAPER BAGS

Materials

Heavy brown paper bags or heavy brown wrapping paper;
White glue;

Soft wire and wire cutter;
Acrylic or tempera paint in fall colors;
Brown marker;
Paint brushes;
Scissors;
Pencils;
Clear acrylic spray if desired for shiny finish.

To Do Ahead—Director or Volunteers

Cut leaf templates from patterns (Figure 2-8). If skills are very limited, use the simpler pattern. Trace the same size as the given pattern.

Directions

1. Place two pieces of brown paper together (may staple together so they won't slip) and draw around the chosen leaf pattern (they may be varied).
2. Cut the leaves out. Cut the two pieces at the same time so they will exactly match. You might mark numbers on the matching leaves so you will always know which ones fit together.
3. Draw the dark lines on the veins of the leaves with brown marker.
4. Cut a piece of soft wire to fit down the center of the leaf, plus extra for stem. If you want a really flexible leaf and the skills of the workers are adequate, cut small cross wires as shown in the small drawing (Figure 2-7).
5. Run a line of glue down center of leaf and across the center line if you are using cross wires. Place wires in the right position and fit the other half of the leaf on top, adding a line of glue around the outside edge of the leaf.
6. Press down firmly, weight down with heavy book and let dry several hours.
7. The leaves can be made very attractive by adding color, gold, red, orange or brown and bending into a natural shape.
8. Spray with acrylic spray for a little gloss if desired. This should be done out-of-doors.

Use or Display

These are nice in antiqued containers or baskets for fall table decorations or used on fall bulletin boards.

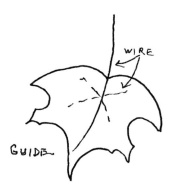

2-7 Pattern

2-8 Pattern

23

Therapeutic Value

Ideas and creativity—choosing colors and painting;
Physical stimulation—hand and arm dexterity;
Social value—conversation, helping others;
Sense of self-worth—contributing to making home more beautiful or decorating bulletin board;
Memory orientation—remembering the falling leaves and colors of fall, and the tasks that were
   done in the fall season.

HANDPRINT POSTERS OR PICTURES

Materials

Sheets of white construction or watercolor paper at least 16 × 20 or 18 × 24 inches in size;
Liquid acrylic paint or liquid tempera. Red or blue are best colors;
Shallow trays or dishes for the paint, large enough for a person's hand to lay flat in the paint;
Poem (included—have as many copies made as you have workers);
White glue;
Wet paper towels or rags for cleaning hands.

To Do Ahead—Directors or Volunteers

Make copies of poem. If some volunteer does calligraphy, these can be beautiful, but typing will
do. This activity must be supervised by director or volunteers.

Directions

1. Pour out enough paint to cover bottom of tray or dish.
2. Have the senior press the right hand flat in the paint. Be sure hand is down as far as it will go.
   If hands are very arthritic you may be able to print only part of the hand: do not let that be
   disturbing, just print all you can.
3. Then press the right hand with the paint on it down as flat as possible on the right-hand side of
   the paper to leave a print. Clean hand carefully.
4. Press the left hand in the paint and lay that hand flat on the left side of the paper (see Figure
   2-9). Both hands may be pressed on one side and poem attached to other side instead of in the
   center.

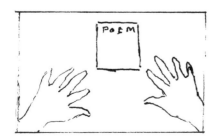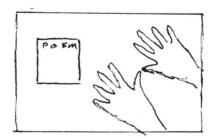

2-9 Arrangement for Hands Poster

5. Lift painted hands straight up when printing to make clear prints, and immediately wipe hands clean. These paints are nontoxic but should not dry on hands.
6. Let paint dry thoroughly. Glue poem in place as shown in drawing.
7. Mount picture on a matboard backing. May be framed.

Use or Display

These make wonderful, appreciated gifts for families.

Hands

Old hands are beautiful to me
They've seen so much of life.
They've soothed a baby's fevered brow
And quieted children's strife.
They've fixed a thousand meals a year,
And washed and ironed the clothes
They've kept a home all neat and clean,
And gardened, canned, and sewed.
Now, they're gnarled and wrinkled, too,
Not glamorous to see,
Their touch still gentle, filled with love,
They're beautiful to me.

Evelyn Lowman

Therapeutic Value

Ideas and creativity—let residents choose which color to print;
Physical stimulation—hand dexterity, pressing hands down tightly against paper;
Social value—cooperation with volunteers and group;
Sense of self-worth—sensing the importance of one's hands, being able to give an appreciated gift to family.

NATURE PRINTS

Materials

Nature print paper—not very expensive, see Appendix for source
Natural materials or man-made objects for printing
Large flat dish for water to set print

To Do Ahead—Director, Volunteers, or Seniors

Able seniors will enjoy collecting some of the materials for this project. Weeds, flowers, leaves, butterflies, sticks, seed pods, or other outdoor findings are charming to use. Cardboard cut out in any shape desired, or other collectible objects can be left on the paper to make a picture.

Directions

1. Place an object, natural or cut out, on the sun-sensitive paper, arranging the objects in a pleasing design.
2. Leave the paper and the objects on it in the sun for the suggested time given on the package.
3. Remove objects and immerse print paper in dish of tap water for a few minutes.
4. These make lovely blue and white prints.

Use or Display

Use to decorate bulletin boards or person's rooms, make designs on cards or give the prints as gifts.

Therapeutic Value

Ideas and creativity—arranging of materials on paper;
Physical stimulation—gathering leaves, flowers, seed pods;
Social value—fun together outdoors and indoors, conversation;
Sense of self-worth—making something lovely to give as gift or to use in the home or in rooms;
Sensory stimulation—feeling the natural materials.

FINGER PAINTING

Materials

Finger paint—can be bought, but is expensive. Finger paint can be made by adding a small amount of powdered tempera paint to clear liquid starch.
Finger-paint paper—fairly inexpensive if you prefer to buy. A substitute for this paper is white shelf paper wet with a damp sponge before using.
Flat dishes or lids for holding paint.

To Do Ahead—Director and Volunteers

Provide bibs to protect clothing and plenty of wet cloths or paper towels for hand cleaning. Also pad the table with newspapers or plastic covering.

Directions

1. Pour desired colors of paint into flat dishes and dip fingers into the paint.
2. Paint with the fingers, the hands, the side of the hand or scrape with the fingernails. A swirling motion is pretty.
3. Let the workers do anything they want with the paint as long as they keep it on the paper.
4. Set finished paintings aside to dry for several hours or overnight.
5. Mount finished paintings on poster board or construction paper.

Use or Display

Use in seniors' rooms or for an art show.

Therapeutic Value

Ideas and creativity—using chosen colors and painting with highly individual technique;
Physical stimulation—hand and finger dexterity and eye-hand coordination;
Social value—conversation and working together;
Sense of self-worth—creating a lovely picture to be used in rooms or for an art show.

CREPE PAPER FLOWERS

POPPIES FROM CREPE PAPER

Materials

Red and black crepe paper and small piece of green for calyx and leaves;
18-gauge floral wire or other heavy wire for stems;
Spool of soft white wire;
Small ½ inch plastic foam ball for center, or substitute several cotton balls wrapped in the black
    crepe paper;
Green floral tape;
Scissors;
White glue.

To Do Ahead—Director or Volunteers

Cut petals if participants are limited in skills. Cut soft binding wire into 6-inch pieces.

Directions

1. Cover the plastic ball or cotton balls with a 2-inch square of black crepe
   paper and twist around the stem wire to hold, adding a bit of glue.
2. Bend a 15-inch heavy stem wire in half and pierce through a plastic foam
   ball (or substitute cotton balls for the plastic), twist ends of wire together to
   form stem (see Figure 2-10).

2-10 Guide—Ball
and Stem Wire

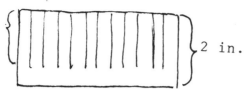

2 in.

2-11 Guide for Stamen

2-12 Guide—Stamen around Center

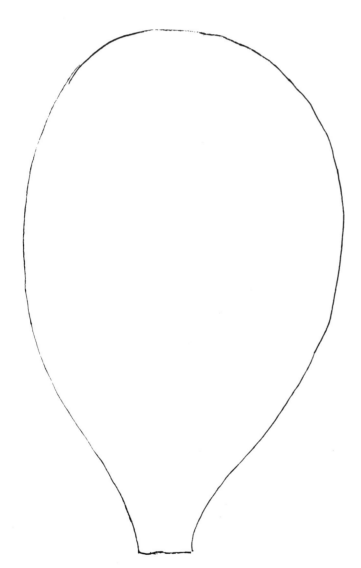

2-13 Poppy Petal—Actual Size

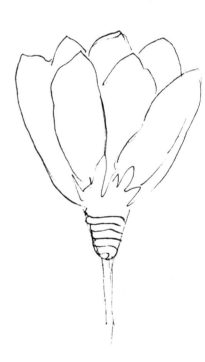

2-14 Guide

3. Cut a 2-inch strip across the end of a package of black crepe paper, leave it folded and cut fringe about 1½ inches deep as shown in guide (Figure 2-11)

4. Unfold the fringed paper so you have one long piece, and beginning with one end work the fringed stamen around the stem using about one-third of the strip, center the covered ball and wrap the base of the gathered paper with thin soft wire, twisting ends of wire tightly together to hold (see Figure 2-12)

5. Cut a 5-inch strip of red crepe paper across the end and cut petals by the pattern shown, actual size (Figure 2-13)

6. Flute the edges of the petals down about one inch and shape the petals to look natural.

7. Arrange six or seven petals around the black stamen and center, overlapping the petals some at the base.

8. Wrap with the soft wire to hold petals in place, adding a little glue if necessary (Figure 2-14).

9. A green calyx can be cut from the pattern, slipped up the stem beneath the petals and glued on (Figure 2-15).

10. Cut leaves from green paper and wind them in as you cover the wire stem with floral tape, starting just under the flower and going to the end, wrapping in the wire covered base and calyx (Figure 2-16). These become easy to make as you work.

Use or Display

Poppies are beautiful table decorations in vases or baskets or even in clay pots made by the seniors. Using the poppies to decorate for a party helps seniors feel needed and proud of their work. Poppies may also be used in residents rooms.

2-15 Calyx—Cut 1 Actual Size

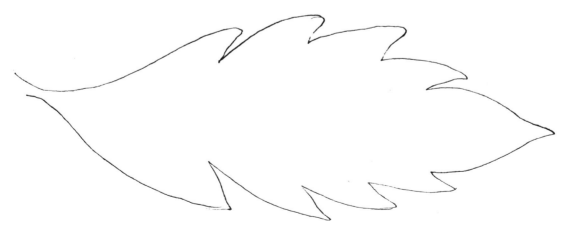

2-16 Leaf—Actual Size

Therapeutic Value

Ideas and creativity—participants will soon discover their own way to work;
Physical stimulation—takes good eye-hand coordination and hand and arm muscles;
Social value—cooperation, helping others less able to work;
Sense of self-worth—contributing to a party in the home or to the beauty of the tables or rooms.

SIMPLE PAPER CRAFTS

FOLDED PAPER CHAINS

Materials

A rectangle of fairly thin paper, such as lightweight drawing paper or bond paper;
Sharp pencils;
Stapler or paper clips;
Scissors;
Colored markers.

To Do Ahead

Fold paper in half through center; fold in half again; and fold a third time to make eight pieces or folds. Enlarge patterns.

Directions

1. Draw half a figure from the patterns given (see Figures 2-17 through 2-23), enlarging to size desired. Provide a template so the residents can draw around it. If skills are limited, volunteers should do this.
2. **Place the figure so the arm or connecting area is at the original center fold.**
3. Hold the folds together with paper clips or a few staples. Then carefully cut around the drawing and open it up to find four joined figures. You can make several strings of them if you need more than four.
4. Draw any needed lines on the figures with colored markers. The Santa (Figure 2-18) should be cut from red paper, and the white beard and trim, black boots, and gloves should be added.

Use or Display

These make interesting decorations for bulletin boards at various times of the year: little girls for a Maypole; Santas or Christmas trees for chains on the Christmas tree; rabbits for Easter, etc.

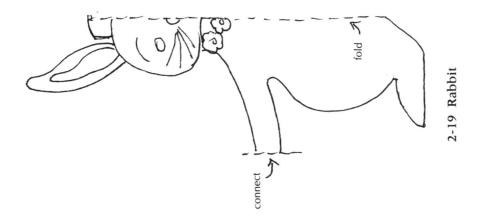

2-19 Rabbit

fold

connect

2-18 Santa

fold

connect

2-20 Bird

connect

fold

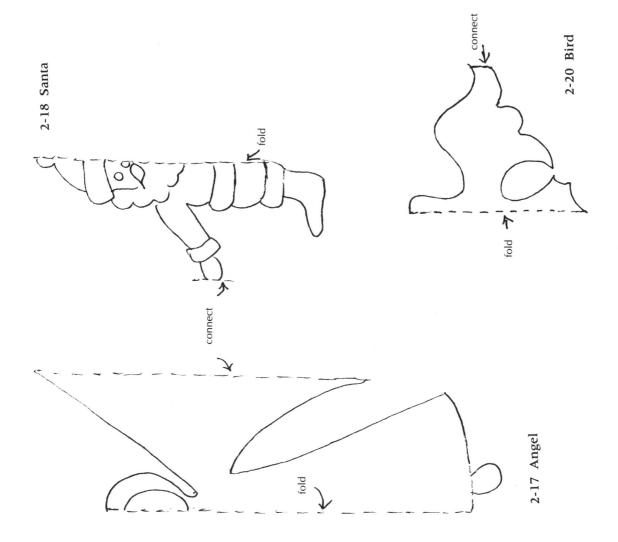

connect

fold

2-17 Angel

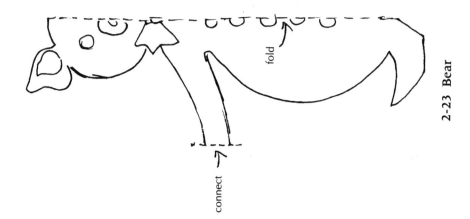

2-23 Bear

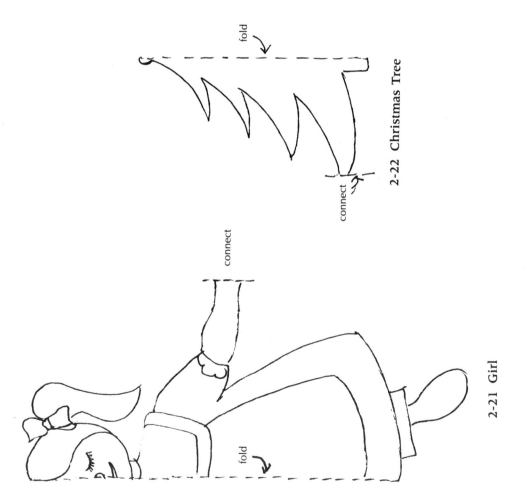

2-22 Christmas Tree

2-21 Girl

Therapeutic Value

Physical stimulation—hand and finger dexterity;
Social value—conversation about the past and cooperation;
Sense of self-worth—making chains for public display;
Memory orientation—most will remember cutting chains for their children;
Reality orientation—relating to the season; Christmas, May Day or Easter.

SILHOUETTES

Materials

Black and white 12 × 18-inch construction paper—See appendix;
Small scissors for delicate cutting—these should be sharp and used only by director or volunteers;
Glue;
Bright light (projector) to cast a shadow;
White pencil.

To Do Ahead—Director

Have light and subject's chair or wheelchair in proper position for shadow.

Directions

1. Put the light about six to eight feet away from the subject.
2. Tape or pin the black construction paper on the smooth wall.
3. Seat the resident in profile position between light and a smooth wall.
4. Turn on light to throw a shadow on the black paper.
5. Trace carefully around the shadow of subject with the white pencil.
6. Carefully cut out the shadow with sharp scissors and glue on the white paper. The director or volunteer should do this.
7. Put the name of the subject on the back of the silhouette.

Variations

Don't let subjects see the finished silhouettes and later let them try to identify their own or to guess who's who. This is great fun.

Use or Display

These make wonderful gifts for families, and are nice on the bulletin board nearest to resident's room.

Therapeutic Value

Ideas and creativity—a means of self-expression;
Physical stimulation—very little for subjects;
Social value—group interaction;
Sense of self-worth—seeing and recognizing one's own picture; satisfaction of giving gifts to family or of seeing one's pictures and those of others on bulletin boards.

CRAFTS WITH PAPIER-MÂCHÉ

PAPIER-MÂCHÉ: METHOD NUMBER ONE

Materials

Papier-mâché paste—Recipe for homemade paste: 2 cups water, ¾ cup flour, 3 teaspoons white glue, or buy Ross paste in powder form to mix with water—it is nontoxic and will keep indefinitely without refrigeration;
Newspapers or other papers; soft tissues; tissue paper; any soft absorbant paper;
Vegetable oil—very small amount;
White spray paint—to be used only by director or volunteers;
Acrylic or tempera paints;
Brushes;
Clear acrylic spray—used by director or volunteers;
Wet paper towels or rags for cleaning hands.

To Do Ahead—Director or Volunteers

Mix homemade paste by stirring a little flour at a time into water, continuing until mixture is the consistency of cream; add white glue. Any leftover paste should be stored in the refrigerator. When ready to reuse, add water a little at a time until mixture is again like cream.

Directions

1. Tear ½-inch strips of newspaper with the grain, top to bottom. For covering large objects, tear 1- or 2-inch strips.
2. Dip strips in the paste mixture, wetting it thoroughly; build up three to six layers on an oiled mold or form. The form can be a metal or plastic object with no sharp corners, or a plastic bowl, an egg, or balloons. The form should be slightly oiled with vegetable oil before gluing so it can be easily removed when the strips are dry.
3. Dry for at least 24 hours, remove from form and sand with fine sandpaper if the article needs smoothing.
4. Spray with white paint and let dry. Then paint with acrylic or tempera paint, decorating in any desired design. Let dry.
5. When thoroughly dry, spray with clear acrylic spray, if you wish to preserve the article. This is done by volunteers.
6. Be sure hands are cleaned often with wet towels.

Variations

Many discarded bottles and containers, or boxes and bowls can be covered with papier mâché to make lovely decorative articles. See ideas below, but add your own.

PAPIER-MÂCHÉ NAPKIN RINGS

Materials

Paper towel tubes;
Papier-mâché paste or Ross paste;
Newspapers;
White glue;
Scissors—sharp craft knife for use by director only;
Acrylic paints;
Trims such as small leaves; pictures; small artificial flowers or fruits; small shells; cords; braids; buttons; sequins;
Clear acrylic spray.

To Do Ahead—Director or Volunteers

With craft knife cut the paper towel tubes into 1½-inch rounds and make the papier-mâché paste. Have participants tear paper into ½-inch strips.

Directions

1. Cover the paper towel rounds with papier-mâché using method number one; let dry about 24 hours.
2. Paint with acrylic or tempera paint in desired color.
3. Glue on trims chosen by the workers. Try to create a pleasing pattern as shown in the guide.
4. Let dry thoroughly for 24 hours and spray with clear acrylic spray to preserve the napkin rings (Figure 2-24)

2-24 Napkin Rings

Use or Display

These are most successfully used when teamed with a set of four napkins such as the ones suggested in Part V, "working with fabrics." They are wonderful gifts for family.

Therapeutic Value

Ideas and creativity—self-expression in choice of materials for one's creation;
Physical stimulation—concentration; eye and hand coordination; use of arm and hand muscles;
Social value—conversation, cooperation with others and helping others with less skill;
Sense of self-worth—sharing and giving gifts bring satisfaction.

PAPIER-MÂCHÉ CANDLEHOLDERS

Materials

Small (½ lb.) soft margarine containers with lids;
Tacky glue;
Craft knife—to be used only by director or volunteers;
Newspapers and papier-mâché paste (made or bought);
Small piece of heavy cord;
White acrylic paint or white spray paint—to be used by director or volunteers;
Gold spray paint or any other color desired—to be used by director or volunteers;
Paintbrushes, if necessary;
Candle, 10-inch.

To Do Ahead—Director or Volunteers

Tear newspaper strips to a 2-inch size and cover work area. Use papier-mâché method number one.

Directions

1. Turn small tub bottom side up; cover the upturned tub and lid separately with papier-mâché strips until about three layers are built up on the forms.
2. Place the lid over the upturned tub evenly, with rim side down (see Figure 2-25); glue together and let dry.
3. With the craft knife (director) cut a hole through both pieces of the covered plastic in the exact center of the top, making the hole to fit the base of a regular 10-inch candle.
4. Glue a piece of heavy cord around the hole.
5. When all is thoroughly dry, paint with white acrylic paint or spray with white paint. You may spray with gold paint instead, if you wish.
6. Decorate with acrylic paints in any design desired.
7. Place candle in hole, pushing to the bottom to hold it securely; this shortens candle to the proper length for the size of the holder.

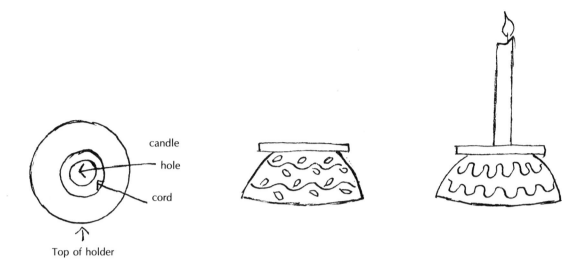

2-25 Guide—Candleholder

Variations

Cover other small boxes, bottles, and containers.

Use and Display

Lighted candles are not used in nursing centers, but can look pretty as a table decoration. They also are much appreciated gifts for family and friends.

Therapeutic Value

Ideas and creativity—self expression by painting any design chosen on the candle holders;
Physical stimulation—good eye-hand coordination and concentration;
Social value—conversation, cooperation with others;
Sense of self-worth—sharing gifts with family and friends; providing decoration for tables.

PAPIER-MÂCHÉ: METHOD NUMBER TWO

Materials

Tacky glue or white glue
Newspaper or other soft papers such as tissue paper or soft tissues (torn in ½-inch strips). The soft papers look prettier on small projects such as jewelry;
Pastry brush or other flat brush for applying glue to any small base;
Wet paper towels for cleaning hands.

To Do Ahead

Residents can tear paper into **small, short, ½-inch strips** and have then ready for use. The beauty of this method for small projects is that the material will remain flexible and can be shaped with the fingers.

Directions

1. Provide a base to work on. This may be an egg, a design cut from lightweight cardboard—anything small will do.
2. Spread glue evenly on the paper and apply to the base.
3. Place another piece of paper on top of the glued strip and press down firmly with the fingers. Add another layer of glue with the brush, add another piece of paper. Continue doing this for four or five times.
4. Be sure the entire base is covered with four or five layers of the glued paper and smooth them carefully with the fingers each time a layer is applied.
5. Let the pieces set about 20 minutes. While paper is still damp and flexible, cut into any desired shape—leaf, flower petals, butterfly or jewelry shapes.
6. Since the paper is flexible, continue shaping as it dries and begins to hold its shape.
7. Let the project dry overnight. Then paint and decorate as with the preceding method, finishing with clear acrylic spray.
8. See the jewelry designs in Part III, "clay." Jewelry pieces can have a pin attached to the back, or a finding for an earring attached, or a hole punched for hanging around the neck with a cord.
9. This is the papier-mâché method to be used with most small projects.

PAPIER-MÂCHÉ FALLOVER EGGS

Materials

Blown-out egg shells;
Tissue paper;
White glue;
Transparent tape;
Very small metal screws or other small heavy metal pieces;
Acrylic paint;
Clear acrylic spray;
Permanent markers in desired colors.

To Do Ahead

Volunteers or friends may be asked to blow out eggs. Blow out the egg shells by making a small hole at the blunt or larger end of shell; prick with a needle at the small end of shell to make hole to blow through. Have one egg or more eggs for each worker. Use papier-mâché method number two.

Directions

1. Close the larger hole at the blunt end of the egg with a piece of transparent tape.
2. Enlarge the hole at pointed end so it is large enough to drop in about a ½ teaspoon of glue and three small pieces of metal. Set aside until dry and metal is held firmly.
3. Close the top hole with a small piece of transparent tape.
4. Tear up small ½ inch squares of tissue paper and glue to surface of egg in four or five layers, letting each layer dry some before applying another. Smooth with fingers.
5. When last layer is dry, apply a thin coat of white acrylic paint. When dry, paint faces on the egg surface (see Figure 2-26.)
6. When these eggs are knocked over, they spring upright.

Use or Display

These make wonderful gifts for children and can be sold at a craft fair. Most older people find them as much fun as children.

Therapeutic Value

Ideas and creativity—creating one's own designs for faces using the given ideas as patterns;
Physical stimulation—hand dexterity and eye-hand coordination;
Social value—conversation, group interaction and sharing help;
Sense of self-worth—satisfaction of creating something for fun, contributing gifts to others.

2.26 Pattern for Face Designs

EASTER EGGS

Materials

Colored plastic eggs or real eggs, enough for each resident to dye or decorate several;
Acrylic paint;
Small brushes;
Easter egg dyes;
Scissors;
Tacky glue;
Small stick-ons of various sizes and shapes—stars, circles, hearts;
Very narrow ribbons, small scraps of lace, or other materials such as sequins, buttons, tiny artificial flowers;
Plastic containers for mixing dyes.

To Do Ahead—Director or Volunteers

Put out the mixed dyes with dippers at hand, and all decorative materials. Have real eggs hard boiled.

Directions

1. For the dyed boiled eggs, let the less able dip the eggs in the various colors and the more skilled do the decorating.
2. The dyed eggs may be decorated with any of the suggested materials using a small bit of tacky glue, or stick-on designs may be used. The workers may also paint on the eggs with acrylic paint (Figure 2–27).
3. The plastic eggs may be opened and filled with small candies and then decorated as shown in the guide.

Variation

For an Easter egg hunt, gold or silver eggs may be hidden with the colored ones; the child or children who find those get a candy bunny.

Use or Display

Use eggs in Easter baskets made by the seniors or use for table decorations. The plastic eggs make lovely gifts for grandchildren.

Therapeutic Value

Ideas and creativity—contributing one's own ideas for decorating eggs and choosing colors; self expression;
Physical stimulation—hand dexterity, eye-hand coordination;
Social value—group interaction; giving aid to those less able;
Sense of self-worth—satisfaction of sharing eggs with children, contributing to the group with table decorations;
Reality orientation—recognizing Easter season.

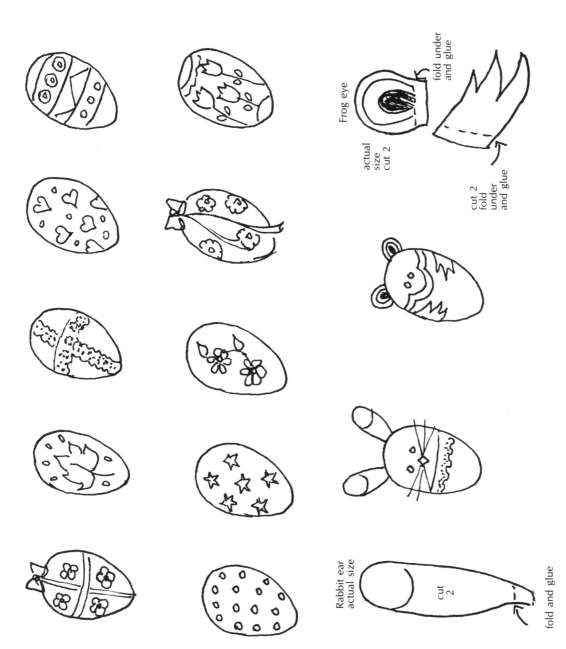

Frog eye

actual size
cut 2

fold under
and glue

cut 2
fold
under
and glue

Rabbit ear
actual size

cut
2

fold and glue

2-27 Guide to Egg Designs, Using Cut-Outs, Decals, Stick-Ons, and Tiny Ribbons, and Lace

COLLAGES AND SPIRALS

COLLAGE—A SENSORY EXPERIENCE

Materials

Papers of various textures—wax, tissue, smooth plastic, pebbled, velour, crepe, textured packing materials, sandpaper;
Fabrics of various textures—felt, brocade, satin, velvet, corduroy, burlap, canvas;
Trim—cords, braids, laces, ribbons, buttons, velcro;
Scissors;
White glue;
Poster board or cardboard for a stiff base. For a more permanent project, use chipboard;

To Do Ahead—Director or Volunteers

Make up a collage as an example and have all materials on the table.

Directions

1. Let each person choose materials and colors to work with, but be sure they choose a *variety* of textures.
2. Papers can be torn into shapes and fabrics can be cut, some making pieces large and some small, using many different shapes.
3. Glue the materials down on the cardboard base in a design pattern pleasing to the workers. It doesn't really matter about proper design patterns as this project is for *feeling*.

Use or Display

Many residents find running their fingers over the various textures pleasing to the senses. They will probably like the soft applications most.

Therapeutic Value

Ideas and creativity—satisfaction of choosing the materials one likes to work with in making a collage;
Physical stimulation—use of fingers, hands, and arm muscles for cutting and tearing shapes;
Social value—cooperation with group, providing help for those with less skill;
Sense of self-worth—satisfaction of providing something for less able residents to enjoy, contribution to the group;
Sensory stimulation—providing a feeling experience for seniors.

SPIRAL DECORATIONS FROM HEAVY CARDBOARD

Materials

Poster board, white or colored;
Round object, such as a plate, about 7 or 8 inches in diameter to use as a pattern;
Scissors;
Small amount of fishing line or heavy thread;
Previously made decorations to suspend from the spiral;
Gold or silver paint for Christmas spiral, if desired.

To Do Ahead—Director or Volunteers

Spray paint the cardboard if using for Christmas. Cut 10-inch squares of poster board and, using the plate as a pattern, draw spiral lines on the square as shown in guide. Draw the lines about ½ inch apart (Figure 2-28).

Directions

1. Have ready or have participants make attractive decorations to attach and hang from various points on the spiral (see Figure 2-29).
2. Cut carefully on the drawn lines of the spiral, cutting in ½ inch from bottom edge of cardboard to get to spiral lines.
3. When cut, the cardboard spiral will drop down as a spring. Attach a small piece of fishing line to top of spiral as shown.
4. Use patterns in bulletin board section to make seasonal decorations, such as shamrocks, hearts, fruits, leaves, pumpkins, bells, angels, etc.

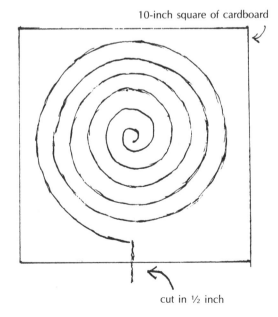

10-inch square of cardboard

cut in ½ inch

2-28 Guide—Spiral Decorations

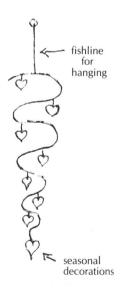

fishline for hanging

seasonal decorations

2.29 Guide for Hanging

Use or Display

Attractive in rooms on in many parts of the center as seasonal reminders.

Therapeutic Value

Ideas and creativity—satisfaction of choosing the designs to be hung on the spirals and the colors
   to be used;
Physical stimulation—hand and finger dexterity required for cutting carefully;
Social value—conversation, group interaction, cooperation;
Sense of self-worth—satisfaction in adding to the beauty and interest of the home.

MOBILES

Materials—for all mobiles

Nylon fishing line;
Assorted papers—tissue, art, cardboard;
Small pieces of bamboo, balsa, ¼-inch dowels, tree branches for hanging;
White glue;
Scissors;
Acrylic paint;
Paintbrushes;
Gold or silver spray paint (use only out of doors).

To Do Ahead

Choose a mobile or mobiles for the seniors to construct and have all materials ready on tables.
Volunteers put mobiles together.

Directions—for All Mobiles

1. Cut out all design parts and put together. Directions for each mobile are provided with the
   drawing.
2. To hang a mobile, always find the balancing point before adding further branches, wire or
   bamboo.
3. Use small pieces of fish line to hang the mobiles from crosspieces.

Use or Display

Beautiful and interesting for any spot in the home, mobiles are especially good for bedridden
patients, giving them something to look at that moves and turns in the air. Mobiles can bring peace
of mind to the restless.

Therapeutic Value

Social value—provides a sense of community;
Self-esteem—contributing to others;
Physical stimulation—hand and eye coordination;
Mental stimulus—provides eye interest, movement, and color to the bedridden.

FISH MOBILE

Materials

Cardboard or art paper—green or blue;
Scissors;
Glue;
Wiggly eyes;
Fishing line;
Suspending materials—balsa, bamboo strips, or branches.

To Do Ahead—Director or Volunteers

Have a finished pattern to show the workers and cut the blue or green paper into 1½-inch strips.

Directions

1. Cut the strips into varying lengths, depending on the size of the fish wanted.
2. Cut the strip half way through on two opposite sides to make the tail (see Figure 2-30).

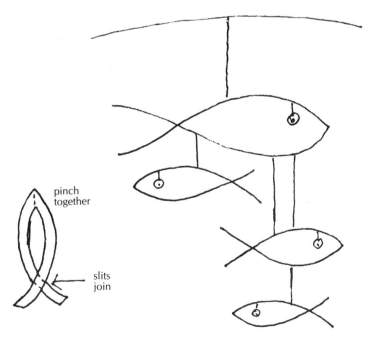

pinch
together

slits
join

2-30 Fish

3. Slip the slots into each other and glue to hold.
4. The eye can be two bought wiggly eyes glued together with a short bit of fishing line glued between them for suspending.
5. The whole mobile is hung from the suspending material with fishing line. Be sure to find the balancing points.

Use or Display

Mobiles can be hung anywhere in the nursing home and are wonderful for use with the bedridden.

Therapeutic Value

The values are the same for all mobiles.

FLYING DUCK MOBILE—BLUE TEAL

Materials

Light cardboard or art paper—blues, greys, or browns;
Scissors;
Acrylic paint or colored markers;
Paintbrushes;
Suspending materials—branches, balsa, or bamboo strips, or
Fishing line for suspending.

To Do Ahead—Director or Volunteers

Enlarge patterns to the size desired and place on the work table for the workers to draw around.

Directions

1. Draw around the pattern, marking where the slit will be cut.
2. Cut the pattern from the grey, blue, or brown paper and carefully cut the slits in exactly the right places.
3. Slip the slits into each other to form the wings of the duck. Bend the wings up or down just a little to make the bird look more real.
4. The beaks and eyes can be painted with acrylic paint or marked with colored markers (see Figure 2-31).
5. Suspend the ducks on fishing line from balsa, bamboo, or wood strips. Be sure to find the balancing points.

Use or Display

These mobiles are beautiful anywhere in the home, but are especially good for the bedridden, suspended where their eyes can follow the movement and color.

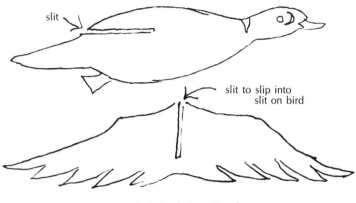

2-31 Flying Duck

Therapeutic Value

The values are the same as for all mobiles.

JOY MOBILE FOR CHRISTMAS

Materials

Poster board or heavy paper;
Foil paper for covering the letters or gold or silver spray paint for covering the letters;
Scissors;
Fishing line;
Suspending material—balsa or wood strips.

To Do Ahead—Director or Volunteers

Have patterns for letters ready "Noel" or "Peace" may also be used if you want several different mobiles (Figure 2–32).

Directions

1. Draw around the chosen letters and cut from poster board or other heavy material.
2. Either spray paint the letters with gold or silver paint or cover with foil paper in red and gold, green and gold or blue and silver—whatever fits your color scheme.
3. Hang with fishing line from the suspending material, being careful to find the balancing point.

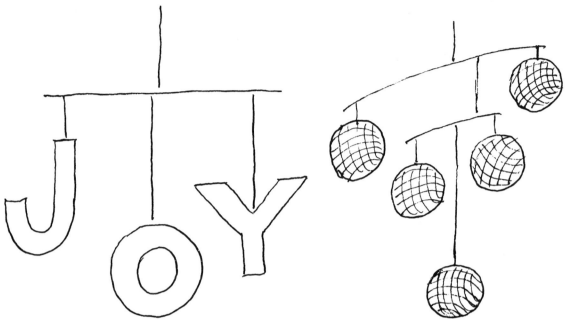

2-32 Joy Mobile for Christmas   2-32 Ribbon Mobile

Use or Display

Hang the various messages throughout the facility at Christmastime.

Therapeutic Value

The values are the same as for all mobiles.

RIBBON MOBILE

Materials

Small balloons, 4–6 inches inflated;
Oil, small amount;
Ribbon or braid;
Papier-mâché paste or white glue;
Fishing line;
Balsa or branch crosspieces for suspending material.

To Do Ahead—Director and Volunteers

Blow up the small balloons to a 4–6-inch size.

Directions

1. Oil the balloons slightly.
2. Cut pieces of ribbon long enough to fit around the balloon.
3. Dip the ribbon in papier-mâché paste or white glue until soaked; crisscross over the balloon. Leave to dry overnight.
4. In the morning, pop the balloon and remove from the ribbon. The ribbon will remain stiff, forming a sphere.
5. Tie a piece of fishing line to the top of each sphere and hang the spheres from the balsa or branch crosspieces. Everyone will wonder how it was done. The ribbons may "give" as you remove the balloon but will spring right back to form a spherical shape.

Use or Display

This mobile is a conversation piece hung anywhere in the center; it is especially nice for the bedridden.

Therapeutic Value

The values are the same as for all mobiles.

Variations

Small "eyes of God" made as directed in Part V, but woven on short sticks or toothpicks, make beautiful mobiles, especially if the yarn used is very colorful. Suspend with fishing line on balsa wood crosspieces.

Butterfly mobiles are also lovely. Make the butterflies using the pattern given in Part VIII, gluing small pieces of wire down the body and across the wings so wings can be shaped in natural fashion. Suspend as usual.

Small sea shells and sand dollars also make lovely mobiles. If using sand dollars, spray with clear acrylic spray so they will not break easily. Hang them as suggested above. You will think of many more ways to suspend interesting materials to make mobiles—almost anything can be used.

STAINED-GLASS TRANSPARENCIES

WAXED-PAPER TRANSPARENCIES

Materials

Broken bits of wax crayons;
Vegetable peelers;
Transparent tape;
Covered ironing board or padded table;
Iron;
Roll of waxed paper;

Black felt-tip pen;
Scissors;
Lightweight cardboard;
Newspapers.

To Do Ahead—Director and Volunteers

Cover table with newspapers. Cut waxed paper to desired size (12 × 12 inches or 12 × 16 inches). Cut designs from cardboard. These can be Christmas decorations, birds, flowers, butterflies, fish, leaves, or anything you choose—you will find patterns throughout this book. Volunteers will do the ironing.

Directions

1. With the peelers, shave about three colors of crayons onto a piece of waxed paper. Let seniors choose their colors, no more than three.
2. Leave about 1½ inches of space all around the edge of the waxed paper with crayon shavings in the center. Place another piece of waxed paper over the shavings to fit the first.
3. Cover the waxed paper "sandwich" with several newspapers, place on padded board or table covered with newspapers and iron at medium heat until shavings melt and run together.
4. Set aside to cool and harden.
5. When they are cool, draw around the cardboard pattern of bird or butterfly with a black felt-tip pen (let residents choose their pattern) and cut out with scissors.
6. Tape artwork in the window (use transparent tape) to catch the light.

Use or Display

This artwork is lovely in windows of residents' rooms or anywhere else in the center. It looks like stained glass and is especially nice to display at Christmas and Easter. This is an easy project for most seniors to make.

Therapeutic value

Self-worth—adding to the beauty of home, room, or center;
Social value—working together with each other and with volunteers;
Mental activity—choosing colors and patterns, generating ideas;
Reality orientation—when used at Christmas or Easter.

3

Modeling Clay and Craft Dough

USE OF MODELING CLAY

Using modeling clay can be a very satisfying exercise for the residents of nursing homes or other care centers. There is something about working with clay that is elemental and therapeutic, and it really does not matter whether the articles created are of great artistic quality or not. The value is in the creating. Self-hardening clay can be obtained from any good craft supply house and is reasonable in price. It can be bought in five-pound cartons or in larger quantities, if desired. This clay requires no firing. Finished products become strong and durable and can be painted with acrylic paint or ordinary tempera paint. Modeling clay must be kept damp, so wrap it in damp cloths when it's not in use and store it in heavy plastic bags, tightly closed.

Kneading clay is the first and primary step in working with clay. This is extremely good exercise for arthritic hands. To knead, move the clay on the outer edges of the portion being worked to the center over and over again. Clay always invites one to touch it and leave the mark of the fingers in it. The very handicapped can simply play with the clay, squeezing it in their hands for its therapeutic value.

Slip must be used to attach one piece of clay to another, smoothing after making each joining. Slip is a mixture of clay and water mixed to the smooth consistency of heavy cream.

SELF-HARDENING CLAY FOR PINCH, COIL, AND SLAB WORK

PINCH POTS FROM SELF-HARDENING CLAY

Materials

Newspapers for covering tables;
Premixed block of self-hardening clay;
Small container of ready-mixed slip;
Cloth or paper towels for cleaning hands;
Container of water for moistening clay;
Tongue depressors or other flat sticks for use as modeling tools;
Rolling pins or one inch dowels cut into twelve-inch lengths for rolling out the clay.

To Do Ahead—Director or Volunteers

Cover the work space with newspapers and be ready to assist with kneading (show them how) and shaping of the clay.

Directions

1. Give each participant a ball of clay about 3 or 4 inches in diameter
2. Have everyone knead the clay until it is soft, pliable and smooth. If this is too difficult, use smaller amounts of clay.
3. When the clay is well kneaded, roll it into a ball shape to make a low, wide bowl or pot, and into a cylinder shape to make a little taller object.
4. Form a depression in the center of the ball with your thumb and keep your fingers on the outside for support.
5. Spread this opening gradually until the sides are uniformly thin, about ½ inch thick. Leave the base thicker than the sides (Figure 3-1).
6. The edge of the bowl or pot opening may show cracks which need to be worked together with wet fingers or by adding thick slip and smoothing it out with the hands or a modeling tool (tongue depressor). Do *not* apply too much water.
7. The finished bowl or pot can have designs incised in it with the end of the modeling tool or can be decorated with thinned acrylic paint when the piece is totally dry. Drying takes several days.

Use or Display

Pots or bowls can be used to hold small items, jewelry, coins, etc., and to make personal space more attractive. They may also be exhibited in a display area or in an art show.

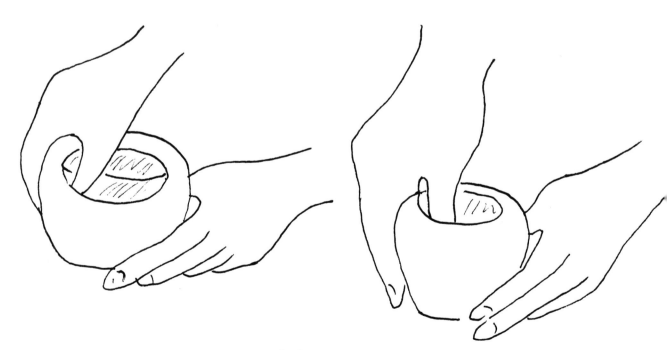

3-1 Guide for Pinching Pots

Therapeutic Value

Ideas and creativity—choosing shapes and decorating in a personal way;
Physical stimulation—wonderful use of muscles, eye-hand coordination;
Social value—conversation, cooperation (more able seniors help less able ones);
Sense of self-worth—decoration for rooms, giving as gifts, exhibiting in an art show;
Sensory stimulation—the feel of clay is most important to workers.

COIL POTS FROM SELF-HARDENING CLAY

The Indians of the Southwest made many coil pots; the shapes and decorations they used are quite beautiful. Books on this subject can be found in any library.

Materials

Newspapers for covering tables;
Premixed block of self-hardening clay;
Small container of ready-mixed slip;
Cloth or paper towels for cleaning hands;
Waxed paper for rolling coil;
Container of water for moistening clay;
Tongue depressors to use as modeling tools;
Rolling pin or one-inch diameter dowel for rolling clay in slabs.

To Do Ahead—Director and Volunteers

Cover the work area with newspapers and be ready to assist with the kneading and shaping. Prepare the slip.

Directions

1. Roll out a small piece of clay into a slab about ½ inch thick and cut a round pancake from it for the bottom of pot.
2. On a board or waxed paper roll a small ball of clay to make long coils. These are rolled with the palm of the hand. Continue to roll with the ball of the hand until the coil is about ½ inch thick. Make the first coil to fit around the cut bottom of the pot, join the ends with a little slip, and with the fingers work the base and coil together carefully.
3. Make a large stack of coils before starting work on the pot.
4. Add another coil on top of the first and continue adding coils, shaping the pot by the length of coils used (Figure 3-2). Use a little slip on the joints but *never* place the joints directly above each other; stagger them.
5. Work all the coils together very carefully and smoothly. The outside can be smoothed with a modeling stick and the finished shape may be a bowl or pot.
6. If you wish to add a handle, as for a cup or pitcher, roll a coil a little thicker, apply at the proper place for a handle and very carefully work the coil into the pot with slip (see Figure 3-3).

7. The inside of the bowl (Figure 3-4) or the outside of the pot (Figure 3-5) can be decorated with thinned acrylic paint when fully dry. Paint a design, stripes, or geometrics similar to those found on Indian pots.

Use or Display

Use in rooms as a decorative item, give as a gift, or use in an art show.

Therapeutic Value

Ideas and creativity—choosing item to make and colors for decorating; also choosing a design for the pot or bowl;

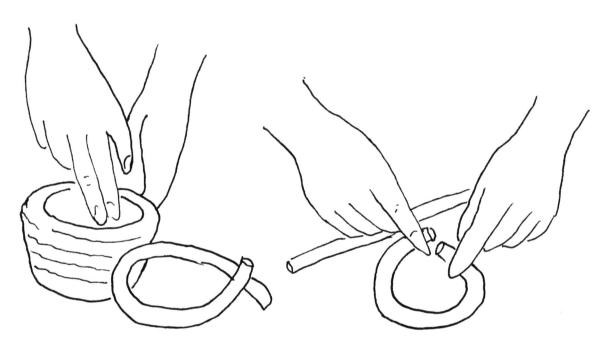

3-2 Guide for Coiling

3-3 Cup Shape and Handle   3-4 Design—Inside of Bowl   3-5 Design on Pot

Physical stimulation—use of arm and hand muscles, hand-eye coordination;
Social value—cooperation with those less able, and conversation about Indian use of bowls and pots;
Sense of self-worth—providing decorations, gifts, contributing to the group and to an art show;
Sensory stimulation—the feel of clay is most important to those who participate.

SLAB POT FROM SELF-HARDENING CLAY

Materials

Newspapers for covering tables;
Premixed block of self-hardening clay;
Small container of ready-mixed slip;
Cloth or paper towels for cleaning hands;
Container of water for moistening clay;
Tongue depressors to use as modeling tools;
Small bit of heavy wire for hanging (if creation is a wall piece);
Rolling pin or one-inch dowel cut in 12-inch lengths for rolling;
Stamping objects—see following section on stamping;
Table knife for residents to cut shapes, or sharp knife for volunteers.

To Do Ahead—Director or Volunteers

Cover work space with newspapers. Be ready to help with kneading and cutting out of shapes with knife. Prepare slip for joining.

Directions

1. On several layers of newspaper, using a rolling pin, roll a 3 or 4-inch ball of clay into a flat ½-inch pancake.
2. Turn the clay frequently to avoid sticking and stick a pin in any air bubbles that appear.
3. Cut to any desired shape from a cardboard pattern such as a fish shape, heart shape, round or oblong shapes (Figure 3-6).
4. The slabs can be joined to make a larger sized piece by moistening the edges and placing the two clay slabs together, adding slip and rubbing and smoothing until the seam will hold. Slab pots are harder to create than pinch and coil pots and tend to pull apart as they dry, if the joints are not properly constructed. The joints should be slightly scored and joined with slip (Figure 3-6).
5. Press a small wire loop into the back of the piece before drying, if the piece is to be used as a wall hanging.
6. Flat rounds or shapes such as hearts may have the edges pulled up slightly and fluted and designs stamped into the bottom of the shape. See stamping directions below.
7. Some of the slab pieces may also have designs cut into the sides as well as being stamped. This stamping and cutting must be done while the pieces are flat and before they are joined.
8. Some of the items that may be made by the slab method are mugs, boxes, trays, low bowls, small planters and lids for other containers, flat, decorative wall hangings such as weed pots, wind chimes, dominoes, jewelry belts, and tokens for a tick-tack-toe game.

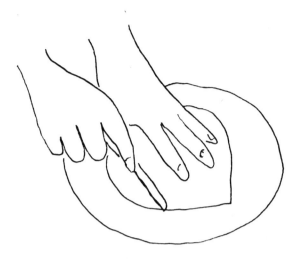

Cutting a heart shape from a slab

Joining a slab

Cut designs in pots can hold a votive candle

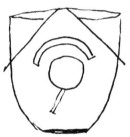

Wren house, coiled or slab,
with sides cut away and slab roof added

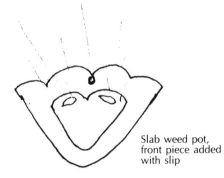

Slab weed pot,
front piece added
with slip

Slab weed pot,
front piece added
with slip

¾ inch in diameter
Token for Tick-Tack-Toe game,
round cut from slab with biscuit cutter

Garlic-press hair added to slab face

3-6 Guide for Slab Pots

Use or Display

Slab projects may be used in rooms or elsewhere in the center; to give as gifts; to display in an art show.

Therapeutic Value

Ideas and creativity—choosing items to make and selecting ways to decorate the creations, using either cutting or stamping;

Physical stimulation—use of arm and hand muscles, hand-eye coordination;

Social value—discussion of creations and how to decorate; cooperation with others; and helping others less able;

Sense of self-worth—making beautiful items for use in rooms, as gifts, or for display in an art show or the center;

Sensory stimulation—the wonderful feel of clay is important.

STAMPING, CUTTING, OR APPLYING DESIGNS IN CLAY

Designs may be pressed or stamped into the clay with a pointed or rounded modeling stick, a nail file, coin, button, key, pencil eraser, pizza cutter, cheese grater, round cap, or other round or square objects. A drinking straw may be used to punch small round holes in the clay. Many materials may be pressed into the clay to give texture; seed pods, leaves, a stiff brush or comb, heavy lace rolled on top of the clay with a rolling pin. Many kitchen utensils will make interesting designs in the clay.

Designs may be cut through the sides of clay pots or bowls with a knife or with the end of a modeling stick. Rounds may be cut with a small biscuit cutter or other small cutter. They may be punched using various sizes and shapes of objects with an edge sharp enough to make a hole.

Designs may also be applied by pinching off small bits of clay, shaping them as desired, and applying them with a bit of slip to the surface of the pot, bowl or slab pieces. Slip kept in a covered jar is necessary for applying all clay decorations to the clay pieces.

Clay can be put through a garlic press to make small strings for hair which can be applied to the heads of figures on the pots.

PROJECTS TO MAKE WITH SLAB CLAY

Materials for All Projects

Newspapers for covering tables;
Premixed block of self-hardening clay;
Small container of ready-mixed slip;
Cloth or paper towels for cleaning hands;
Container of water for moistening clay;
Tongue depressors to use as modeling tools;
Rolling pin or one-inch dowel for rolling clay;
Objects used for stamping;
Table knives for cutting.

Added Materials for Wind Chimes

Cords for hanging;
Straws or other punching tool for punching holes;
Hanging rings—macrame supplies;
Weights, such as heavy books, to weight down slabs.

Added Materials for Dominoes

Pencils with erasers for pushing in holes, or making dots;
Weights as above.

Added Materials for Bowls Made on Forms

Forms to drape clay over, such as small plastic bowls in various sizes;
Vegetable oil for oiling forms;
Stamping materials.

Added Materials for Making Belts

Small punching tools, such as straws;
Thin leather strips or heavy cords for joining clay pieces.

WIND CHIMES

Directions

1. Roll out a ball of clay in a slab ¼-inch thick. From this slab, cut a round 6–8 inches in diameter. This is for the piece that the cords run through (see Figure 3-7).
2. Punch as many holes as you want to have hanging chime pieces for and cut a different length cord for each one but of a length that allows them to touch slightly so they will chime in the breeze. Weight down clay and allow to dry.

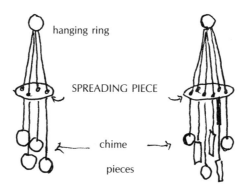

3-7 Wind Chimes

3. From the remainder of the same slab cut as many small pieces as you cut holes for in the "spreading piece." These will form the chimes and can be cut in any desired shape—rounds, triangles, shells, butterflies, leaves, flowers, etc. Weight down the pieces and allow them to dry thoroughly.

4. Tie all the cords to a hanging ring with a knot and run the other end of the cord through the punched holes in the spreading piece.

5. The chime pieces can be decorated in any desired way, with applied designs or painted designs in bright colors. Use acrylic paint for this. Then tie the chime pieces to the ends of the cords.

DOMINOES

Directions

1. Men love this project. Roll out a slab of clay, ¼-inch thick and cut the domino rectangles, all the same size, from the slab. Press a line in center of rectangle.

2. Press the white dots in the proper places with the eraser end of a pencil. Weight down the pieces and allow to dry thoroughly. This sometimes takes several days.

3. The pieces can then be painted with acrylic paint. First paint the dominoes black, red, dark green, or blue; then paint the dots white (Figure 3-8).

4. Always place newspapers over and under the clay to dry. The papers and the weight keep them from warping. It is nice to make these dominoes a little larger than usual.

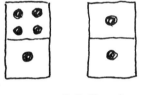

3-8 Dominoes

BOWL FORMED WITH SLAB CLAY

Directions

1. Provide a small plastic bowl to use as a form; oil the bowl so the slab can be easily removed when dry.

2. Roll out a slab of clay ¼ inch thick, cut to a size to fit over the bowl shape. Press the clay firmly against the oiled form. Cut away excess clay at the edge of bowl. If desired, decorate with incised shapes.

3. Cover the clay with damp newspapers and allow to dry. This may take several days. Check frequently to see if cracks appear. If they do, repair them with slip and smooth again.

4. When the bowl shape is thoroughly dry, it can be painted with acrylic paint (Figure 3-9).

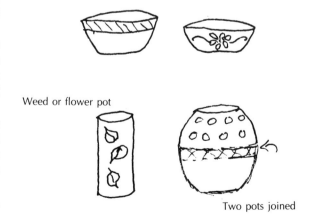

Weed or flower pot

Two pots joined

3-9 Small Bowl Shapes Made over Plastic Bowls

5. Two small bowls may be placed together by turning one over the other to form a hollow piece. These can be quite imaginative.

BELTS FROM SLAB CLAY

Directions

1. Roll out the clay into a ¼ inch slab and cut out the shapes you like. These can be rounds, oblongs, or rectangles (see Figure 3-10).
2. Punch holes with a straw or other punching tool in the four corners of the cut-out shapes and add a small applied piece of clay for decoration.
3. Run a thin leather strip or heavy cord in a suitable color through the holes as shown in drawing. Bring the ends of the cords or strips through a clay bead which has been rolled into a ball with a large enough hole punched through it to receive the cords. Tie the cords securely at the end.

Use and Display for all Projects

Most of these slab projects can be used in the center for decoration, in the rooms of residents and to give as gifts. Some may be used for art shows.

Therapeutic Value

Ideas and creativity—all clay work is creative for everyone involved in choosing designs, which projects to make, and decorating them.
Physical stimulation—use of arm and hand muscles and eye-hand coordination.
Social value—conversation, cooperation with others and helping those with lesser skills.
Sense of Self-worth—making lovely items to play with, to decorate with, to wear, gives a feeling of self-esteem.
Sensory stimulation—being exposed to the wonderful feel of clay.

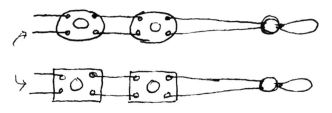

3-10 Belts to Make

CRAFTS WITH BAKER'S CLAY DOUGH

BAKER'S CLAY DOUGH ORNAMENTS

Materials

4 cups flour
1½ cups salt
1½ cups water
¼ cup liquid oil

Mixing Directions

Mix together flour and salt in a bowl. Mix water and oil and add gradually to the salt and flour mixture until dough is formed. Turn out on a lightly floured board and knead until smooth, adding a litte water if dough is too stiff. This dough will last indefinitely in the refrigerator, but after storage you may need to add more flour. To use, keep dampened washcloths or paper towels handy so dough will not dry on hands. Knives, cutters, acrylic paint, and brushes are the items needed for this project.

To Do Ahead—Director or Volunteers

Mix dough and have ready on covered tables.

Directions

1. Roll dough out about ¼ inch thick and cut designs by using a knife or cookie cutter, by stamping, or by molding by hand. Punch small hole near top of piece for hanging.
2. Decorate with small shaped pieces of dough, but do pieces that are *not too thick*.
3. Bake on foil-covered cookie sheet at 300 degrees until hard.
4. Objects can be painted with acrylic paint to make Christmas ornaments, hearts for Valentine's Day or any other design you might want to try.

Use or Display

Ornaments can be used on Christmas tree, in seniors' rooms, to give as gifts. They might also be displayed at an art show.

Therapeutic Value

Ideas and creativity—deciding on the design to be made and how to color or decorate it, self-expression;
Physical stimulation—use of arms and hands, eye-hand coordination;
Social value—conversation about Christmases past and the types of ornaments people had or made; cooperation, helping others who are less skilled;
Sense of self-worth—sharing with others in the home; giving ornaments as gifts;
Memory orientation—remembering other Christmas times and becoming oriented to the time of the year.

CRAFTS WITH GLUE DOUGH

GLUE DOUGH RECIPE

This is a more dense clay material that doesn't have to be baked, but must be allowed to dry thoroughly.

Ingredients

½ cup flour
½ cup cornstarch
½ cup Elmer's Glue-All

Mixing Directions

In a bowl, mix and knead all dough materials until blended. If mixture is too dry, add more glue, a drop or two at a time. If it is too moist, add a little flour and cornstarch very carefully. Dough will keep for weeks in a tightly closed bag in refrigerator.

Materials for All Glue Dough Recipes

Glue dough (see recipe above)
Knife for cutting;
Rolling pin or 1-inch dowel;
Pencil or toothpicks;
Water in small container for attaching clay pieces;
Acrylic paint;
paint brushes;
Clear acrylic spray;
Shells large enough for a spoon rest, to use as a form;
Drinking straw for punching holes, or other punching tool;
Small pink cord or ribbon for lacing heart.

Directions for Place Cards

1. Roll out a ½-inch thick piece of glue dough and cut out an oval or rectangular shape for the place cards (Figure 3-11).
2. Press in the letters with the sharp point of a pencil or a toothpick.
3. Form small flowers from clay and attach with slip or water; let dry.
4. Paint the background of the oval place card blue with a white border; paint lavender flowers and green leaves, or any colors desired, using acrylic paint.
5. Make a small wedge as shown (3-11), cut from the clay, cutting it at a slight slant so the place card will stand. Attach to back of place card. When all is dry, spray with acrylic spray to protect.
6. The **Christmas place card** is made the same way, but roll out the clay to ¼ inch thickness and cut a rectangle (Figure 3-11).

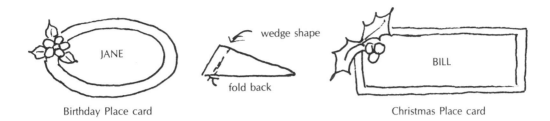

3-11 Guide for Place Cards

7. Press in the letters in the same way; make holly leaves and berries from small pieces of clay, and attach with slip or water.
8. When all is dry, paint the background with white acrylic paint, paint the letters in red, the holly leaves green, and the berries red.
9. Attach wedge, cut on a slant as above, to the back of place card. When dry, spray with clear acrylic spray for protection.

Directions for Shell Spoon Rest

1. Oil a shell large enough to provide a rest for a spoon.
2. Roll out a piece of clay ¼ inch thick and press it over the shell and into its crevices. Cut clay off around edges, smooth edges, and let dry.
3. Paint with acrylic paint, pale pink, peach, lavender, or tan. When it is dry, spray with clear acrylic spray (Figure 3-12).
4. Use any other fruit or vegetable shape to make a spoon rest.

3-12 Shell Spoon Rest

Directions for Laced Heart

1. Cut a clay heart from a piece of glue dough ¼ inch thick.
2. Punch holes around the edge, placing them ½ inch apart, use a drinking straw or other punching tool (Figure 3-13).
3. Paint the heart red and lace the edge with small pink cord or ribbon. Makes a wonderful Valentine gift.

3-13 Laced Heart

Use or Display

The place cards can be used on birthday tables or Christmas tables. The spoon rest and laced heart make wonderful gifts or can be displayed at an art show.

Therapeutic Value

Ideas and creativity—choosing colors; doing one's own designs for flowers, etc.; self-expression;
Physical stimulation—use of arms and hands, hand-eye coordination;
Social value—conversation; visiting; cooperation; helping others who are less skilled;
Sense of self-worth—contribution to family and friends for birthdays and Christmas; contribution to the nursing center as a whole; giving gifts.

SIMPLE CLAY MAGNETS AND NAMETAGS

Materials

Self-hardening clay or glue dough;
Rolling pin or 1-inch dowel;
Small 2-inch biscuit cutter for round shapes;
Table knife;
Ruler for cutting other shapes;
Acrylic paint;
Paint brushes;
Tacky glue;
Waxed paper;
Stick-on decals;
For name tags, ¾-inch pin clasps with safety catches;
For magnets, strip of magnet paper or small magnets;
Fine line waterproof marker;
Clear acrylic spray.

To Do Ahead—Director and Volunteers

If using glue dough, have the recipe mixed. If using self-hardening clay, spread the table with newspapers and prepare slip.

Directions

1. Knead self-hardening clay, if using instead of glue dough.
2. Roll either type clay out evenly and quite thin, no more than ¼ inch thick. Cut rounds or geometric shapes as desired. Smooth edges.
3. Place on tray covered with waxed paper; put waxed paper over the shapes and set aside to dry with slight weight on top.
4. When dry, paint with acrylic paint and let dry again.
5. Decorate magnets with decals and write names on the name tags with any color fine line waterproof pen.
6. Glue pin clasp to back of name tag and glue magnet to back of the decorated clay piece.
7. Spray with acrylic spray, to make charming magnets or name tags.

Variation

If you want a decorative pin instead of a name tag, the pin can be decorated with bits of clay, decals, or small pictures before spraying with clear acrylic spray.

Use or Display

Name tags can be given to volunteers or worn at special occasions. Small magnets make nice gifts for family and friends.

Therapeutic Value

Ideas and creativity—choosing decals and colors can be a form of self-expression.
Physical; stimulation—use of muscles in arms and hands in kneading, eye-hand coordination.
Social value—cooperation, contribution to the group and helping others less skilled.
Sense of self-worth—sharing with others in family and with friends brings self esteem.

CLAY KEY CHAINS

Materials

Self-drying clay or glue dough;
Rolling pin or large dowel, waxed paper for rolling clay;
Two-inch biscuit cutter for cutting round shapes; table knife and ruler for cutting squares, triangles or rectangles.
Acrylic paint in desired colors;
Paint brushes;
Water or slip for wetting edges;
Key chains from craft supply;
Decals for decorating;
A punching tool or drinking straw for making the holes in clay.

To Do Ahead-Director or Volunteeers

Cover work area with newspapers; have towels for cleaning hands. Mix glue dough if using. Pre-mix slip if using self-hardening clay.

Directions

1. Knead clay, if using self-hardening clay
2. Roll either type of clay out to a ¼ inch thickness on waxed paper.
3. Cut rounds with biscuit cutter, or cut other shapes with knife held along edge of ruler. Punch hole large enough for key chain.
4. Smooth edges with wet finger, cover with waxed paper, and weight down with a light weight when drying. This takes at least a day.
5. When dry, paint with bright colors and let dry again.
6. Stick on chosen decals and spray with clear acrylic spray.

Use or Display

These are wonderful gifts for friends or family.

Therapeutic Value

Ideas and creativity—choosing decals and colors for self-expression;
Physical stimulation—eye-hand coordination; muscles used in kneading;
Social value—conversation; cooperation; helping those who are less able;
Sense of self-worth—gift giving and sharing help self-esteem.

JEWELRY FROM MODELING CLAY OR GLUE DOUGH

Materials

Clay—self-hardening or glue dough;
Cords and ribbons for necklaces;
Jewelry findings for pins and earrings;
Acrylic paint;
Paint brushes;
Punching tool or drinking straw for making holes in clay;
Items that can be used to imprint designs, such as cords, shells, leaves, round cutters;
Table knives for cutting out shapes;
Rolling pin or large dowel for rolling clay;
Tacky or white glue;
Water or slip for moistening joints;
Damp rag for cleaning hands.

To Do Ahead—Director or Volunteers

Knead the clay—or help the residents do it—until clay is soft and pliable. Cover work area with newspapers; prepare slip.

Directions

1. After kneading, roll the clay into a flat shape about ¼ inch thick. If you wish to imprint a design, simply press the shape (shell, leaf, cutter) into the clay until the imprint is deep enough.
2. After cutting all the shapes needed for the piece of jewelry (Figures 3-14, 3-15), smooth the edges with a dampened finger or slip.
3. Tiny pieces of clay, rolled in the hand to form a roll, may be applied to the clay slabs by moistening the base piece and pressing the applied form to it, smoothing edges.
4. When project is finished to your satisfaction, punch any holes in the clay if it is to be a necklace and put aside on wax paper to dry thoroughly. Weight the pieces down so they dry without warping.
5. Paint with acrylic paint and let dry again. Spray with clear acrylic spray to protect and give gloss.
6. Finally, run a cord, ribbon, or leather strip through the holes made for the necklace, glue a pin clasp on the back if making a pin, or glue an ear clasp on if making an earring.

3-14 Guide for Jewelry: Necklaces

Use or Display

Residents can wear the jewelry or give as gifts. Jewelry can also be displayed at an art show, or used for bingo prizes.

Therapeutic Value

Ideas and creativity—choosing the item one wants to make and choosing the proper design are forms of self-expression;
Physical stimulation—kneading is good for both arms and hands;
Eye-hand coordination in putting the jewelry together is beneficial;
Social value—conversation; cooperation with others is always helpful to the one who gives aid.
Sense of self-worth—wearing a personal creation, sharing with others, and having one's creation used in the nursing home as a prize or in some display builds self-esteem.

3-15 Guide for Pins and Earrings

4

Batik, Tie-Dye, and Rubbings

BATIKS TO MAKE WITH PAPER

DRIP DESIGN ON PAPER

Materials

Heavy white drawing paper or construction paper;
Small eyedroppers;
Poster paint or liquid acrylic paint;
Colored art or construction paper on which to mount the paintings;
White glue.

To Do Ahead—Director or Volunteers

Fold the heavy white paper in half crossways.

Directions

1. Give each participant a small eyedropper and have them drip the paint in small dots and a few squiggly lines on one half of the folded paper only. Be sure to use colors that look good together.
2. Fold the paper back together and press with hand to create a beautiful abstract design. Use very little paint and do not have it too thick. **Drip means drip.**
3. Drops of paint can also be flung on white or light colored tissue paper to make gift wrap paper. These make lovely abstracts.

Use or Display

Nice for room decorations when mounted on colored paper to complement the colors used in the painting. Une on bulletin board or in an art show.

Therapeutic Value

Ideas and creativity—self-expression in color and design;
Physical stimulation—eye-hand coordination;

Social value—conversation, cooperation;
Sense of self-worth—contribution to the home, one's rooms, or art show.

DESIGN WITH CRAYONS ON PAPER

Materials

Lightweight shelf paper, drawing paper, or any other lightweight white paper. Light colors may
   be used instead of white;
Wax crayons in assorted colors;
Vegetable peelers;
Newspapers;
Iron and ironing board or heavily padded table.

To Do Ahead—Director and Volunteers

Cut paper to desired size; pad ironing board with newspapers. Ironing will be done by volunteers.

Directions

1. Fold the cut paper in half.
2. Lay unfolded paper on table and shave crayons (in colors chosen) with the vegetable peeler.
   Put the shavings only on one half of the paper and use only two or three colors per picture.
   Use small amounts of crayons and leave about 1½ inches of paper without shavings around
   the edges.
3. Fold the other half of paper over the shavings.
4. Place the paper with shavings folded inside on the newspaper-covered ironing board; add one
   or two sheets of newspaper on top and press with a very warm iron, melting and spreading the
   shavings to form a design.
5. Open the paper and let it cool to make a colorful painting.

Use or Display

These make lovely abstract designs that can be used for room decoration if mounted on matboard or art paper. They can also be used to wrap small gifts. They are wonderful for an art
show.

Therapeutic Value

Ideas and creativity—self-expression in choosing colors and in the design which emerges;
   stimulates mind;
Physical stimulation—hand and arm dexterity; concentration; eye-hand coordination;
Social value—conversation; talking about pictures; cooperation with others;
Sense of self-worth—sharing; contribution to the home or one's own room decoration; self-
   esteem from contributing to an art show.

GLUE DRAWING

Materials

White construction paper or watercolor paper;
White glue in small bottles with a spout for individual use;
Watercolors or acrylics in colors that go well together, such as blue and yellow, blue and brown, rose and blue, yellow and orange;
Any simple line design—fish, flower, goose, butterfly, etc. (see Part VIII for designs);
Pencils.

To Do Ahead—Director and Volunteers

Enlarge design on pantograph to desired size. Trace design with a pencil on white paper and run off needed number of sheets on copy machine or, (depending on skill level), make a template and let workers draw around the pattern that they choose.

Directions

1. Have each senior choose a design from the ones drawn on the white paper.
2. Show participants how to outline the design with a thin line of glue, squeezing it from the small bottle with spout.
3. Let design dry completely, probably overnight.
4. Make washes (a mixture of paint and water) of different colors and paint over the glue, which will reject the color. Use enough water to make the colors run together. Selected colors will combine to create another lovely color—blue and yellow combining to make green for the fish; blues and browns combining to make gray for a goose; rose and blue combining to make lavender for the flower; yellow and red combining to make orange for the butterfly. The secret is in using enough water and enough paint to make the colors run together.
5. The pictures can then be mounted on a colored piece of mat board or cardboard to provide a frame for the painting.

Variations

Names can be written in large letters in glue on a piece of waxed paper and sprinkled with glitter. Let dry about 48 hours and peel them off the paper to use on packages. Or use rainbow glue (colored glue) in the same way.

Use or Display

Use as decorations for rooms, for bulletin boards, for art shows. If using glue names, use on packages or to put names on birthday gifts.

Therapeutic Value

Ideas and creativity—self-expression of choosing designs desired; deciding on colors wanted;
Physical stimulation—limited muscle use; eye-hand coordination; hand and arm dexterity;

Social value—cooperation with others; helping others; conversation;
Sense of self-worth—contribution to the home or to an art show; giving a gift to a loved one.

PAPER BATIK

Materials

Sturdy bond paper, construction or art paper, charcoal or watercolor paper;
Wax crayons of any color (large kindergarten crayons are good);
Watercolors or colored inks; black ink, thinned;
Soft brushes;
Iron and ironing board;
Newspapers;
Clean absorbent cloth;
Designs—butterflies, flowers, birds, or star shapes, stripes, various geometric shapes.

To Do Ahead—Director or Volunteers

Have designs enlarged, traced, and ready on table for workers to choose.

Directions

1. Draw the design with crayons in chosen colors on the white paper. Don't let the wax color be too solid.
2. Apply watercolor wash or ink with a soft brush over the entire paper, covering the waxed design. This is called the **roll-off method.** The water-based paint will roll right off the portions covered with wax.
3. Examples of combinations: Flower drawn with desired color with a blue-green wash over it; stripe design in blue, grey, and rose with a dark blue wash; fish or butterfly in yellow or orange with a deep purple wash over; or use a black wash of thinned ink over any of the designs.
4. When water-based paint or ink is dry, place the design on folded newspapers on an ironing board, cover with a clean cloth, and with a warm iron, press the wax out, leaving only the color. A piece of bond paper may be placed beneath the design and on top of the newspapers and the color from the batik will transfer to the paper in a soft blurred duplicate.

Variations

Use a white crayon or candle stump and draw the design on colored paper, then brush with the watercolor or ink. When the wax is ironed off the color of the paper will be preserved.

If your facility can afford some expense, you can order Dippity-Dye paper in packs of 100 sheets, 18×24 inches, along with the Dip n' Dye colors, red, blue and yellow, to mix almost any other color. These are very reasonable in price. The dyes are cold water dyes and nontoxic. The paper is folded or pleated and dipped, again and again, to form wonderful creative designs.

Use or Display

Decorations for seniors' rooms, for gifts, or for display on bulletin boards or in art shows.

Therapeutic Value

Ideas and creativity—choosing designs and colors to use is a form of self-expression; using the mind creatively;

Physical stimulation—hand and arm dexterity, hand-eye coordination;

Social value—cooperation; helping others who are less able; conversation and visiting;

Sense of self-worth—sharing one's contributions with others in the home, on bulletin boards or art shows, or giving as gifts.

TIE-DYE

BASIC TIE-DYEING

Materials

Fabric—muslin, old white sheets, cotton, linen, natural fibers are the best. Old sheets and cotton T-shirts are excellent.

Dyes—Cold water dyes (bought from a craft shop) or other fabric dyes, such as Rit, that can be used in warm water: Hot wax and very hot dyes cannot be used with the elderly;

Plastic or enamel containers in which to mix the dye and dip the cloth, one container for each color dye;

Materials to bind or twist or tie—rubber bands of different sizes, cords, nylon rope, soft wire, masking tape, plastic wrap, pipe cleaners, clothespins, large clips, large bobby pins;

Marbles or pingpong balls can be used to tie into the fabric to form circular designs.

To Do Ahead—Director and Volunteers

Lay the material out on the table and cut into appropriate sizes. Mix the dyes. Show a finished product if possible. Demonstrate tying and wrapping the fabric.

Directions

1. With the available materials, let the residents tie, fold and bind their cloth any way they wish, giving them help as needed. The object is to tie the material in such a way that the dye will penetrate only the outside of the fabric (Figure 4-1).
2. Dip the tied material in the dye and, *leaving it tied*, remove from dye and allow to dry totally. If more than one color is going to be used, start with the lightest color for the first dipping.
3. When the fabric is dry, let the seniors untie it and retie it in a different way.
4. Dip again in a darker color; leave tied; and let totally dry again.
5. Untie and wash according to instructions on the dye.
6. Iron the finished product.

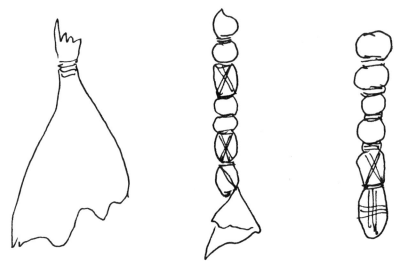

4-1 Wrapping the Fabric

Use or Display

Fabric can be used for decoration in seniors' rooms, down the halls, or on bulletin boards. The dyed fabric can be mounted and hung on the walls or used for an art show. T-shirts can be worn or given as gifts.

Therapeutic Value

Ideas and creativity—a great deal of self-expression is involved in the tying of the fabrics. This increases self-confidence;

Physical stimulation—excellent use of hand and arm muscles; also eye-hand coordination and dexterity;

Social value—conversation and visiting; cooperation; helping each other with the tying of the fabric;

Sense of self-worth—contribution to the nursing center as a whole, to the decoration of the halls and to an art show. The satisfaction of making something that is very interesting and beautiful.

Variations

Tie the fabric with cord, rubber bands, plastic wrap, string, etc.

Accordion pleating the fabric will form narrow stripes. You can also gather pleats with heavy thread and pull up tight, or hold the pleats with clothespins or bobbie pins (Figure 4-2).

4-2 Pleating and Pinning

Tying small round objects such as marbles or ping pong balls into the fabric will make a circular design (Figure 4-3).

For the less able, fabrics can be folded, held with bobbie pins or clothespins, and color dripped on with a large eyedropper or kitchen baster. Drip color directly onto the folds and squeeze. Or the edges of the folds may be dipped in the dye and left to dry. When dry and unfolded, the design remains.

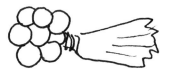

4-3 Tying Round Objects

RUBBINGS

MAKING THE RUBBINGS

Materials

Paper—use lightweight but flexible paper (good quality rag content paper works best). Do not use thick, stiff papers;

Crayons—large, heavy, *flat* crayons in black, brown, dark blue;

Objects for rubbing—many kitchen tools are excellent for rubbing: potato mashers, slotted spoons, grills, or metal baskets, the smooth side of cheese graters. Other objects could be coins, ornate buttons, heavy lace, grainy woods, fern leaves or shapes cut from heavy cardboard and glued down on another sheet or paper and rubbed over.

To Do Ahead—Director or Volunteers

Have an assortment of objects available for rubbing; have paper cut and ready for participants.

Directions

1. Carefully apply the crayons, *broadside,* not with the point. To get the best from your motif, rub it in different ways—sometimes lightly, sometimes heavily, sometimes with a mixture of strokes.
2. If you use cut-out shapes glued down on a backing, wait until the glue is perfectly dry to take a rubbing.
3. You can also cut geometric shapes and glue a series of them on a backing and take a rubbing of it. Generally rubbings are left as they are on the paper but a wash of water and paint can be put over them if you wish to experiment.

Use or Display

These make lovely decorations for rooms or hallways. Change all decorations frequently so they remain fresh. If displayed, they should be mounted on mat board or heavy paper. Excellent for an art show.

Therapeutic Value

Ideas and creativity—choosing an object to rub and learning the technique of rubbing builds self-confidence and fosters self-expression;

Physical stimulation—eye-hand coordination; hand and arm muscle use;

Social value—conversation; working with others to create something beautiful; helping others who are less skilled;

Sense of self-worth—sharing materials; contributing to the center as a whole and to an art show.

5

Weaving, Quilting, and Designs with Fabrics and Yarns

WEAVING ON CARDBOARD LOOMS

LOOM WEAVING

Materials

Inexpensive chipboard looms from a craft supply company (easier than making the looms);
Plastic needles ordered from the same source;
Yarns, strings, cords, in a mixture of textures and colors;
Heavy yarn needle or darning needle;
Cotton string for binding;
Scissors.

To Do Ahead—Director and Volunteers

Order all materials and have them ready for workers.

Directions

1. Some purchased looms have slots or notches and some will have holes punched about ¼"
   apart at each end. If loom is notched, warp by pulling string from one top notch to correspond-
   ing bottom notch; the warp threads are ready for weaving. If loom has holes, a binder cord can
   be used to give closer warp threads. To make a binder cord at each end of loom, tie string to
   one corner, thread it into darning needle and sew in and out through holes across the end of
   loom. When opposite side is reached bring the needle back across the loom, going in and out
   alternate holes to make a continuous binder cord as shown in Fig. 5-1.
2. Begin to warp the loom by tying a 3-yard length of heavy yarn to one corner (see Figure 5-1).
3. Use a heavy yarn needle to bring the warp thread across the length of the loom and through
   the opposite string loop, then back and forth through the loops at each end.

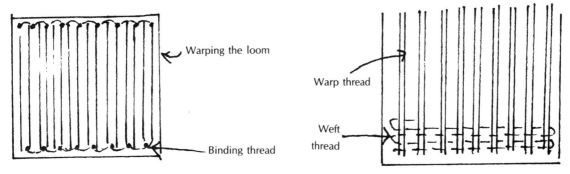

5-1 Guide

4. Tie knots in the warp threads as more warp is needed to cover the entire surface of the loom with double vertical warp. Don't worry about knots as they will be hidden in the weavings.
5. When the loom is warped, carry the weft thread back and forth with the plastic needle or shuttle, pushing the yarn up tightly as you weave.
6. You can use a variety of colors and textures to give the weaving character.
7. When the loom is covered, the cardboard loom is turned over and the binding threads cut from the back so the finished piece can be lifted from the loom. Looms can be used again and again.
8. Remember: Warp threads are vertical; weft threads are horizontal.

Use or Display

Large squares can be used for pillow tops, smaller ones for bulletin boards, or they can be sewed together for wall hangings for halls or residents' rooms.

Therapeutic Value

Ideas and creativity—weaving can be extremely creative in the choosing of colors and textures to use;
Physical stimulation—good use of arm and hand muscles;
Social value—conversation, cooperation with others. This is also an exercise that can be done by the residents alone in their idle time.
Sense of self-worth—contribution to the beauty of the nursing center and the giving of gifts.

EYES OF GOD—OJOS DE DIOS

Materials

Dowels or bamboo sticks for larger ojos, any other straight sticks and toothpicks for very small ojos;
Three to six colors of four-ply yarn (use colors that are pleasing together);
Craft knife for notching sticks (to be used only by director);
White glue;
Scissors;
Paint for sticks if you want them colored.

To Do Ahead—Directors and Volunteers

Cut sticks, if necessary, to proper length and notch in the exact center of each. Glue them together. Cut yarn in manageable lengths depending on size of ojo.

Directions

1. After sticks are measured, cut to desired length, notched, and glued, and are completely dry, start weaving ojo.
2. Start the weaving with a double half hitch knot (Figure 5-2). You will use this knot at the beginning and end of each change of yarn.
3. Start with double half hitch on arm one, tighten the knot, wrap the yarn around the loose end to hold it down and push up to center.

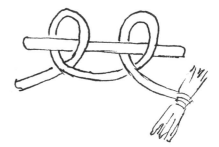

5-2 Double Half Hitch

4. Hold the stick skeleton in your left hand, thumb on center front, with the skein of yarn in the right hand bring the yarn over arm two, then pass it underneath and up around the stick.
5. Push yarn up to center. Encircle arms three and four the same way (Figure 5-3). Keep even tension so the yarn doesn't bunch up.
6. When you change yarn, end with clove hitch and cut the yarn, leaving about ½ inch to be covered by the next round.
7. Start again with a clove hitch, always starting a new color on a different arm from the one just wrapped (Figure 5-4).
8. Use a little white glue on the back of the yarn if it seems to be slipping. Always end a color on the same arm on which you started it.
9. This procedure becomes very easy after a few rounds. The ojo is said by the Southwestern Indians to bring good luck and to protect the home. They can be woven by young and old.

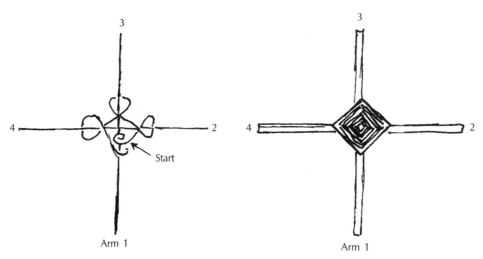

5-3 First Round   5-4 After Several Rounds

Use or Display

Large ojos can be used as room decorations or on bulletin boards. Small ones make lovely jewelry or mobiles, decorations for Christmas trees or gift packages. They can be used in a variety of ways, such as stuck in a foam base for a table decoration.

Therapeutic Value

Ideas and creativity—choosing colors to go together for the ojo;
Physical stimulation—concentration, eye-hand coordination; use of hands and fingers;
Social value—conversation; cooperation; helping others who are less skilled;
Sense of self-worth—contribution to the nursing center; satisfaction of feeling successful; sharing; giving as gifts.

DESIGNS WITH YARN

WHIMSICAL YARN DESIGNS

Materials

Cardboard for base—matboard is excellent;
Art paper or construction paper in light colors—9 × 12-inch size;
Yarns in assorted colors (see pattern for suggestions);
Pompoms in assorted colors—¼-inch size;
Black or brown markers;
White glue;
Scissors.

To Do Ahead—Director and Volunteers

Cut cardboard to fit as a backing for the colored paper. Enlarge desired patterns on the pantograph to any size desired and outline them on art or construction paper.

Directions

1. Glue colored paper (example, red paper for watermelon) with design outlined on it to the cardboard backing, or glue directly on cardboard.
2. When dry, start gluing the yarn to the circular parts of the design in a spiral form until the proper size is reached. Put the glue on only a small portion of the design at a time so it does not dry too quickly. On the watermelon and fish, the yarn may be applied in a straight or zigzag design. See Figure 5-5.
3. Glue on the pompoms at the positions shown in the drawings.
4. Draw the necessary lines with markers and cut the other parts of each pattern from a contrasting color paper.
5. Glue these parts in their proper places.

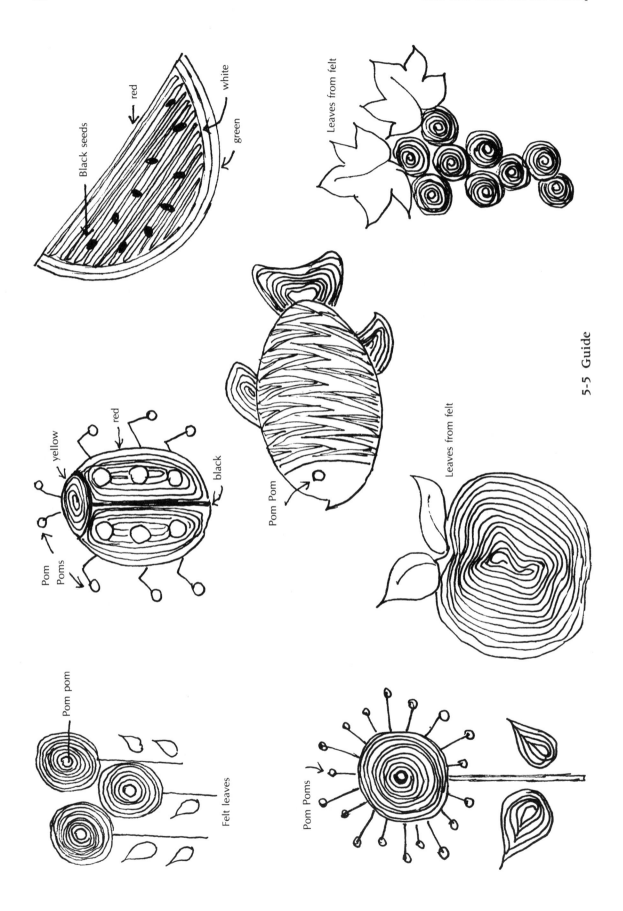

5-5 Guide

Use or Display

These make interesting room or bulletin board decorations or gifts.

Therapeutic Value

Ideas and creativity—choosing the colors one wishes to use and the design desired requires some self-expression;
Physical stimulation—eye-hand coordination and use of arms, hands, and fingers.
Social value—visitation and cooperation; helping others who are less skilled.
Sense of self-worth—satisfaction of sharing, adding to the beauty of the home, and giving as gifts.

WRITING WITH YARN

Materials

Rug yarn or strong white cord;
Waxed paper;
White drawing or bond paper—9 × 12-inch size;
Masking tape;
White glue;
Flat containers for glue (yarn must be soaked).

To Do Ahead—Director or Volunteers

Write the workers' first name on a piece of white paper in black ink; use script writing if possible. Write the name large enough to cover the paper. Cover the writing with a piece of waxed paper and tape it down at the edges.

Directions

1. Pour enough glue in the small shallow containers for two residents to use.
2. Dip the yarn in the bowl of glue, soaking it, then squeeze it out with the fingers and arrange it on top of the name design on the waxed paper. Encourage participants to follow as carefully as possible the curves of the writing.
3. Allow the glue design to dry thoroughly; then lift from the wax paper and glue on a gift package or mount on colored paper. Project can be done in any desired color of yarn and mesages other than names can be used. Try "Merry Christmas," "Happy Birthday," or "I Love You."
4. Any other design can be placed under the waxed paper and yarn soaked with glue can be placed over the design. Some designs can be seasonal, such as a Christmas tree, bell, star, heart, shamrock, butterfly, or pumpkin.

Variations

Rainbow (colored) glue can be used. The glue can also be sprinkled with glitter while it is still wet.

Use or Display

These designs are interesting when used to decorate gift packages, or when mounted on a piece of colored paper or matboard to hang in residents' rooms.

Therapeutic Value

Ideas and creativity—creative when choosing designs other than the residents' name;
Physical stimulation—good eye-hand coordination and use of fingers;
Social Value—conversation about names; visiting; cooperation;
Sense of self-worth—the use of the individual's name gives a sense of self-esteem and makes him or her feel important.

FABRIC DESIGNS

FABRIC POTPOURRI BAGS OR LAVENDER SACHETS

Materials

Fabric, as rich as possible, in 4 × 10-inch rectangles;
Ribbons and laces, gold cord, decorative braids, pretty buttons, sequins, small artificial flowers;
Net in soft color for heart-shaped bag and bags for the handicapped;
Tacky glue;
Potpourri mixture or lavender sachet powder to put in bags;
Cotton balls, if using sachet powder;
Scissors.

To Do Ahead—Director and Volunteers

Have fabric pieces cut in rectangular shape or in heart shape. For the handicapped, cut net squares about 6 × 6 inches to be filled with cotton balls and sachet powder. Roll the cotton balls in sachet powder.

Directions

1. Lay the cut pieces of fabric right side up and glue on any desired decorations, saving ribbons for tying at the neck.
2. Fold crosswise (Figure 5-5) and glue sides together by running a line of glue down each side of fabric and pressing together until dry.
3. Fill with potpourri or lavender and tie at neck. If using sachet powder, fill the bag loosely with cotton balls.
4. Attach a small loop of ribbon through the tie for hanging on a clothes hanger.

For Heart-Shaped Potpourri Bags

1. Cut two matching pieces of net in heart shape.

2. Glue gathered lace to one side of net, around outside edge of heart, and glue matching net over it, leaving a few inches open at top of heart.

3. Add a piece of ribbon or gold rickrack over the glued seam; stuff with potpourri and glue opening shut.

4. Add ribbon bow and artificial flowers at the top of heart, as shown in drawing (Figure 5-5).

5. Add a gold cord loop at top (for hanging) by gluing or catching with a few stitches. These make sweet-smelling sachets for closets.

Use or Display

This project can be hung in closets for a fresh smell, given as gifts, or hung outside each door for a nice smell in the halls.

Therapeutic Value

Ideas and creativity—choosing colors, fabrics, and potpourri scents;
Physical stimulation—good for hands and arms; good eye-hand coordination required;
Social value—conversation and visiting; talking about favorite smells;
Sense of self-worth—sharing with others, making the home smell nice, or giving as gifts.

Variation

Fill small net squares with potpourri or cotton balls rolled in sachet powder and tie at the top with a narrow ribbon. Best for the handicapped.

5-5 Guide

CRAFTS WITH PRINTING DESIGNS

VEGETABLE PRINTS AND LEAF PRINTS

Materials for Vegetable Prints

Vegetables that make a distinct design when cut, such as green peppers, acorn squash, onions, mushrooms, okra, or fruits such as pears, oranges, lemons, apples;
Thick acrylic paint;
One-inch brushes and a very small brush for painting seeds, etc.;
Knife for cutting vegetables and fruits—used only by director;
Newspapers and paper towels for drying vegetables;
Iron and padded board or table for setting paint;
Linen-type fabric, fringed on the edges (see directions for napkins, below)
Small calendars and thermometers (can be ordered) for calendars.

To Do Ahead—Director and Volunteers

Cut the fruits and vegetables and allow residents to choose what they want.

Directions

1. After the vegetables and fruits are cut, dry them well on paper towels.
2. Apply paint liberally on cut side with large brush.
3. Place fruit or vegetable very carefully when printing, holding some parts down with a pencil, if necessary.
4. Press down firmly and very carefully lift cut fruit or vegetable straight up. A heavy pad such as a folded blanket under the fabric being printed makes it print better.
5. When prints are completely dry, iron the back of them to fix the paint so they are washable. (Director or volunteers do the ironing.)
6. Before ironing, seeds or any other small details can be painted with small brush.

Materials for Leaf Prints

Fresh leaves—geranium, sycamore, oak, grape, ivy, fern—any leaf with a distinct pattern (but not a smooth thick leaf that won't lie flat);
Unbleached muslin or linen-weave fabric in natural color, 18 × 18 inches square for pillow tops or about ⅝ yard; for six napkins, each about 14 inches square, you need 1 yard of 48 inch wide fabric, or 1 yard of 60 inch wide fabric for eight napkins. You will need a 12 × 24 inch piece of fabric for the calendars;
Liquid acrylic paint, green, brown, or any other color you choose;
Small flat bristle brush or foam brush;
Brayer (roller) or short piece of 1 inch dowel or rolling pin;
Newspapers, paper towels;
Polyfoam stuffing (if making pillows);
Scissors.

To Do Ahead—Director and Volunteers

Cut fabric to right size for chosen project. Have leaves ready. Some of the residents may be able to enjoy collecting the leaves.

Directions

1. Arrange the leaves, underside up, in a pleasing pattern on scrap fabric.
2. Remove one leaf; lay it textured side up on a piece of newspaper.
3. Using the brush, coat the entire top of the leaf with paint.
4. Carefully and quickly, place the leaf back in position with the painted side down on the fabric.
5. Place a paper towel on top of the leaf; roll brayer over the leaf or use fingers to press firmly so it will imprint.
6. Carefully lift leaf; the pattern will remain. Continue until all leaves have been printed in design desired.
7. When dry, iron the fabric on the back to set the paint, being sure to cover the fabric with a scrap of cloth on the front before ironing.

Directions for Napkins—Avoid Dark Materials

1. Have the squares cut to desired size and pull threads for ½ inch on all sides, making a fringed edge. (Placemats may be made the same way. Threads can be pulled by the workers at various times, alone or in groups)
2. On sewing maching, stitch at base of pulled threads on all four sides. This prevents fraying.

Directions for Pillow Top

1. With right sides (already leaf-printed) facing in, glue decorative ruffling or edging to one side if desired, and stitch the front and back together, leaving a 6-inch opening in one end for stuffing.
2. Turn right side out, stuff with polyfoam stuffing and slip-stitch opening to close.

Directions for Fabric Calendar

1. On 12 × 24-inch fabric, use the above method for printing the leaf or vegetable design.
2. Turn a one-inch hem across the top and glue down so a small stick or dowel can be inserted in the hem to keep the top straight for hanging.
3. Glue on edging instead of pulling edges for fringe.
4. Glue a small calendar and thermometer on the lower part and attach a cord to each top corner for hanging (Figure 5-6).

Variation

Leaves or other flat objects such as feathers, ferns, or cut-out patterns and shapes can be laid on thick, light-colored paper and spattered or spray-painted with a dark color. Lift leaves or other materials and the design will remain.

Napkin

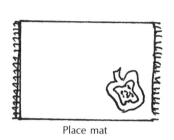

Place mat

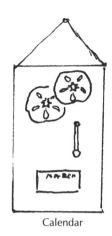

Calendar

5-6 Guide

Use or Display

The napkins can be used with the papier-mâché napkin rings (Part II) to make a wonderful gift or to offer for sale. Pillows and calendars can be used in residents' rooms.

Therapeutic Value

Ideas and creativity—choosing materials and designs, choosing colors and deciding where to apply them on the material encourages self-expression;

Physical stimulation—eye-hand coordination; good arm, hand, and finger muscle use;

Social value—conversation and visitation; helping others who are less skilled;

Sense of self-worth—sharing with others; contributing to the beauty of the center, or giving projects as gifts to family and friends.

TABLECLOTHS FROM OLD SHEETS

Materials

Old sheets, preferably white, but solid colors can also be used successfully;

Liquid acrylic paints;

Brushes in various sizes and foam brushes;

Leaves for printing; vegetables or kitchen tools can also be used to make lovely prints. Try a potato masher, grater, biscuit cutter, spatula with cutouts—any tool that will make a design when dipped in paint. Dip residents' hands in paint and make handprints;

Aluminum pie tins for holding paint;

Scissors;

Iron and padded board or table for setting paint.

To Do Ahead—Director and Volunteers

Cut the sheets to proper size and shape for the tables to be used.

Directions

1. Talk to workers about the designs and allow them to decide on the ones they like best.
2. Decide where to place the designs on the tablecloth.
3. Dip the printing medium in the paint, place it on the cloth in the proper place and press down firmly.
4. Lift the object straight up so it will not smear; let the paint dry.
5. Continue printing until the cloth design is complete.
6. When the cloth is totally dry, iron with a medium iron on the wrong side.

Use or Display

Tablecloths can be used for parties and other special occasions. They can be used with hand-painted white paper napkins if the napkins are made to match.

Therapeutic Value

Ideas and creativity—choosing designs and colors are a means of self-expression;
Physical stimulation—use of arm, hand, and finger muscles; eye-hand coordination.
Social value—conversation, cooperation while doing something together on a larger scale;
Self-worth—contribution to the center as a whole and providing decorations for a party can be very satisfying.

FELT CRAFTS

FELT PILLOWS

Materials

Pieces of colored felt, 12–15 inches square—two pieces for each pillow. Contrasting colors of felt for applied designs;
Fabric glue or tacky glue;
Scissors;
Polyfoam stuffing, enough for the desired number of pillows;
Paper compass, or a round plate or other object of the right size, if making round pillow.

To Do Ahead—Director and Volunteers

Measure the pillow size and mark cutting line on the felt a with fine marker. Cut the shapes to be applied only if the workers are unable to do so.

Directions

1. Pin or staple the two pieces of fabric together and cut the pillow shapes so they will match exactly.

5-7 Felt Pillows

2. Carefully remove pins or staples (volunteers).
3. Put an ample ribbon of glue about 1 inch in from all the edges of the pillow, leaving unglued a space large enough for a hand. This will leave room for stuffing.
4. Press all the edges down well and let dry.
5. When the glue is dry, check to be sure all edges are well glued; stuff pillow with polyfoam through the opening left in the side. Do not stuff too tightly.
6. When you have a nice soft pillow, glue the open space shut and let it dry.
7. Copy a design from any other part of the book and cut from contrasting felt. Make lines on it with colored markers. Cut out and glue on front of pillow. Use designs such as birds, shells, flowers, leaves, faces, fish, butterflies, etc. Make the design large enough to nearly cover the front of pillow (Figure 5-7).

Use or Display

Pillows can be used in residents' rooms, given as gifts, or sold at a craft fair.

Therapeutic Value

Ideas and creativity—choosing designs and colors for self-expression;
Physical stimulation—use of hands and fingers; eye-hand coordination;
Social value—visitation; cooperation with others; helping those with less skill.
Self-worth—sharing with others who might need a pillow and giving as gifts can add to self-esteem.

CHRISTMAS STOCKINGS FROM FELT OR VELVET

Materials

Large pieces of felt or velvet in assorted colors—red, green, white, or brown;
Trims of all kinds—ribbons, laces, braids, sequins, beads, buttons, fake jewels, cords, small bells;
Tacky glue in applicator bottles or small brushes for gluing;
Scissors.

To Do Ahead—Director and Volunteers

Enlarge pattern and cut templates for the stocking, old-fashioned shoe, and boot pattern.

Directions

1. Fold fabric with wrong sides together, and pin to hold in place.
2. Place chosen template on fabric and draw around it with a soft pencil or pen, making a visible mark.
3. Cut through the two thicknesses at one time following the drawn pattern lines.
4. Glue trims on top side of stocking, making them rich and festive (Figure 5-8).
5. Run a line of glue around three inside edges of one stocking piece, leaving top open, and lay the matching piece over it. Weight it down and let dry. This will take quite a bit of glue to hold.
6. The fancy, rich trims are used on the stockings; or you can cut different shapes of flowers from felt and glue on sequins, beads, buttons to decorate the stockings.
7. The shoe can have buttons, gold laces, or braid glued on.
8. The boot can be decorated with black or brown cord for the design, adding some gold trim. This is the place to use your imagination.

Use or Display

These stockings, boots, and shoes can be hung in residents' rooms at Christmas or sold at a craft fair. They also make wonderful gifts for family.

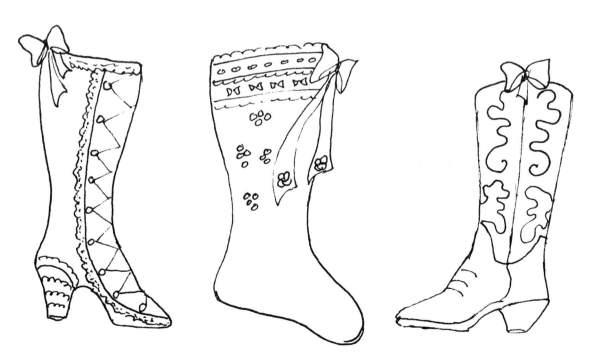

5-8 Patterns for Stockings

Therapeutic Value

Ideas and creativity—choosing designs, colors, and trims;
Physical stimulation—using arm, hand, and fingers, eye-hand coordination;
Social value—conversation; cooperation; helping others;
Sense of self-worth—sharing with those who are unable to make the Christmas stockings; giving as gifts;
Memory orientation—remembering the season of Christmas.

QUILTING—SIMPLE METHODS

PATCHWORK PATTERNS: USING LEFTOVER WALLPAPER OR FABRICS

Materials

Wallpaper samples (for limited skills), or fabric for those with more adequate skills, or those who like to quilt;
Heavy cardboard or mat board;
Pencils;
Scissors;
Tacky glue;
Patterns for patchwork (enlarged);
Bias tape in various colors.

To Do Ahead—Director and Volunteers

Cut cardboard for backing to proper size—12–16 inch squares. Enlarge patterns and duplicate them (Figure 5-9). Glue each pattern on a cardboard square. Let the residents choose the pattern they want to make. For some workers the fabric or paper will need to be cut ahead of the craft session; others will be able to cut their own, using the template pinned to the material or paper. However, the pieces do require accurate cutting.

Directions

1. Help each person who is capable of cutting to trace the template; let them cut the necessary pieces from the wallpaper or fabric.
2. After cutting, the pieces can be glued to the cardboard with the pattern drawn on it, making the quilt square 12–16 inches in size.
3. Bind the edges with bias tape, glued on. These patterns can be quite beautiful if colors are carefully chosen and arranged. Most of the women will have made quilts, which is a plus.
4. If any of the residents are skilled enough, they can piece and sew their blocks, remembering to add ¼ inch on each seam for joining. These could be assembled into 2 × 4-foot blocks, bound on the edges and displayed on nursing center walls.

Variable squares

Checkerboard squares

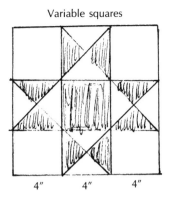

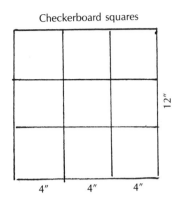

4″   4″   4″

4″   4″   4″

12″

Rob Peter—Pay Paul

Dutchman's Puzzle

Orange Peel

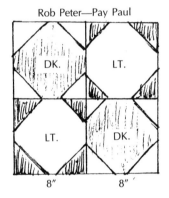

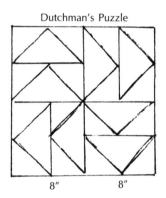

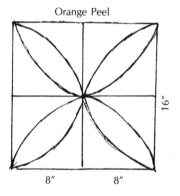

8″   8″

8″   8″

8″   8″

16″

Pinwheels

Double Nine Patch

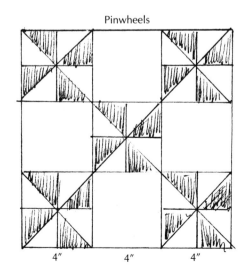

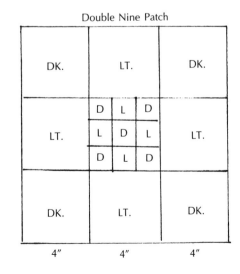

4″   4″   4″

4″   4″   4″

5-9 Patchwork Patterns

Variation

Residents might make cooperative small quilts to give as gifts, to sell at craft fairs, or make smaller quilted squares to use as pillow tops. If residents are not able to quilt, they may be able to tie knots to hold a small quilt together. These can be very pretty and make lovely quilts for small children and babies.

Use or Display

The pieced squares make lovely decorations for residents' rooms, for the rooms and halls of the nursing center, for bulletin boards, and for gifts.

Therapeutic Value

Ideas and creativity—choosing a favorite quilt patterns, choosing colors, and arranging the pieces require concentration and self-expression;

Physical stimulation—using arms, hands, and fingers; good eye-hand coordination;

Social value—conversation about quilts seniors have made in the past; cooperation; and helping others;

Self-worth—providing something of beauty and value to the home; giving gifts to family and friends; creating something which can be sold;

Memory orientation—remembering times past, quilting with old friends, and the patterns that are their favorites.

FEELING BOOKS: A SENSORY EXPERIENCE FOR USE WITH THE HANDICAPPED

Materials

Soft, padded, cloth-covered book about 5 × 8 inches or 8 × 10 inches in size (Check a good variety store);

Collection of materials for gluing on pages—sandpaper, feathers, leather or chamois, lace, heavy yarn or cord, waxed paper, fur and any other textured material available such as papers and packing materials, various textured fabrics such as velvet, corduroy, satin, brocade, burlap, felt, canvas, cotton knits, and also buttons, snaps, zippers, velcro, and any other materials you might desire;

Tacky glue;

Scissors.

To Do Ahead—Director or Volunteers

Purchase the soft book, which should have removable pages. Remove any pages not needed or add extra pages if necessary.

Directions

1. On each page glue one of the various textured materials, after cutting and trimming to proper size for page.
2. If you find that the residents are enjoying the book, make several of them and keep them passed around to as many as possible.

Use or Display

Residents who are unable to participate in the craft program or whose behavior has changed due to Alzheimer's or dementia can often enjoy turning the pages of a book and feeling the various textures of materials. Touching is always an important activity for the aging handicapped.

Therapeutic Value

Ideas and creativity—provided by the director and volunteers and those who assemble the book; Sensory stimulation—provides sensory stimulation for the handicapped; gives them something to do with their hands, to touch and to receive different sensations from the various materials.

6

Projects from Discarded or Throw-Away Materials

CRAFTS FROM DISCARDED KITCHEN MATERIALS AND OLD PANTYHOSE

PLANT OR POPCORN CONTAINER

Materials

Empty 1-quart yogurt containers or similar container;
Small rope, twine, or cord (polyester cord in white is beautiful for Christmas or Valentine's Day);
Two or three colors of cord can be used for fall, such as yellow, orange, and red, with leaves for decorations;
Tacky glue;
Scissors;
Felt in assorted colors for flowers, leaves, hearts, holly;
Trims, braids, small artificial berries, leaves, etc.;
White or colored paint for container—if desired, but not necessary if the yarn or cord is kept close together.

To Do Ahead—Director or Volunteers

Spray paint container if you need them painted; let them dry thoroughly.

Directions

1. Starting at the top of the painted container, put about 2 inches of glue around upper part of the container and start winding the cord or twine.
2. Keep it very close together and continue gluing and winding until the bottom is reached.
3. Glue some kind of decorative braid at the very top of container, or use ribbon.
4. Cut out some of the designs chosen and mount on the side of the container. These designs can be holly leaves and berries, hearts, leaves, flowers, shells, acorns, pine cones—use your imagination. (All decorations can be cut from the felt or can be bought ready-made. (See Figure 6-1)

6-1 Guide

Use or Display

Use as plant, cookie, or popcorn containers. Some can be used in residents' rooms and some of the plant holders could be used elsewhere in the nursing center.

Therapeutic Value

Ideas and creativity—choosing the decorations for the containers and choosing the colors to be used;
Physical stimulation—use of muscles in arms, hands, and fingers; good eye-hand coordination;
Social value—conversation; visitation; and cooperation.
Sense of Self-worth—contribution to the whole; decorative items for rooms; containers to give as gifts.

Octopus from Old Pantyhose

This idea was taken from a picture in a craft catalogue. The original used yarn, but we adapted it and made a much more attractive octopus by using discarded pantyhose.

Materials

Large number of old pantyhose, 12 pair for each octopus;
Heavy string or rubber bands;
Small amount of polyfoam stuffing;
Three yards of 1-inch ribbon or fabric strips for each octopus;
Small pieces of black and white felt for eyes;
Tacky glue;
Scissors;

To Do Ahead—Director or Volunteers

Cut off panty section of hose, leaving the legs to use. Three legs are used for each braided arm.

Directions

1. Cut off the toe of one leg—of the pantyhose measuring up at least 6 inches—to use for the head of the octopus.
2. Secure the three cut ends (cut from panty section) tightly together by tying with heavy string or holding with rubber bands before beginning to braid.
3. Braid the three legs together for one arm and tie at end with ribbon bow. Make eight of these arms.
4. Tie all eight arms together with strong cord or heavy rubber bands and push them up inside the one cut off toe portion. Then, holding them in place, stuff all around the tied ends with poly stuffing to shape the head.
5. When the head is tightly stuffed and is shaped like an octopus head, (see Figure 6-2) tie all parts together tightly at the neck. Tie first with string or cord and then with ribbon bow.
6. Cut the eye parts from black and white felt, glue the parts together as shown; glue them in the proper place on the head.
7. This project is particularly good for those who have use of only one arm or hand: one hand can hold while another person braids.

Use or Display

This is a wonderful gift for a child; or residents may like them for their rooms.

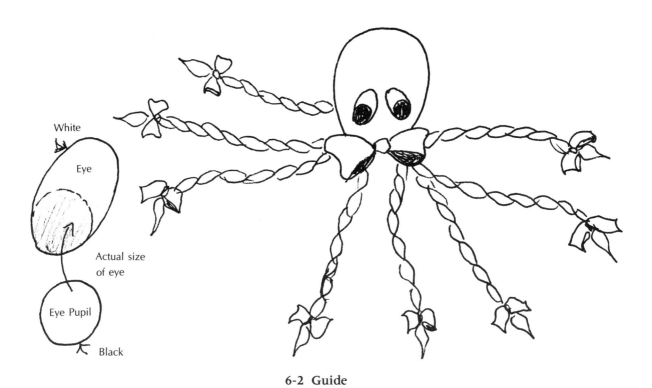

6-2 Guide

Therapeutic Value

Ideas and creativity—all the eyes and braids will be different as participants express themselves.
Physical stimulation—wonderful for arms and hands—even the handicapped can be involved.
Social value—conversation; cooperation; helping others.
Self-worth—giving as a gift to a child or using in one's rooms.

POPCORN FLORALS

Materials

Fresh warm popcorn;
Powdered tempera paint;
Quart-size plastic bag;
White construction or drawing paper for designs; colored construction paper in green or brown
    for leaves and stems;
Colored markers in green and brown (if you prefer to draw in the stems and leaves);
Scissors;
White glue;
Small brushes or cotton swabs for gluing;
Newspapers to cover tables.

To Do Ahead—Director

Have popcorn popped and materials ready on tables. Enlarge the floral designs and have copies
on white drawing or construction paper. These may be run off on the copier. Let residents choose
the designs and colors they like.

Directions

1. Place a teaspoon of powdered tempera in a plastic bag and drop in two or three cups of warm
   popped corn.
2. Fold top of bag and shake well until corn is evenly colored.
3. Help the workers glue the colored corn in a floral design on a white sheet of paper following
   the design (Figure 6-3); when dry, mount on colored construction paper with ½ inch of the
   color showing at edges. Coordinate the colors of the edge and floral.
4. Cut branches and leaves from colored construction paper and glue in proper place or draw
   them on the paper with colored markers.

Use or Display

These are lovely used in residents' rooms or on the hall bulletin boards for everyone to enjoy.
Remind workers not to nibble the popcorn after it is colored (although tempera paint is nontoxic).

Lilac

Bluebonnet

African violet

Geranium

Peach or cherry blossom

6-3 Guide Patterns

98

Therapeutic Value

Ideas and creativity—choosing the design workers like best and choosing the color to be used is a form of self-expression;

Physical stimulation—use of fingers and hands and good eye-hand coordination required;

Social value—conversation about kinds of flowers workers like, cooperation with others;

Self-worth—making something interesting and colorful from popcorn can be a fun experience.

PENCIL AND PEN HOLDERS FROM DISCARDED CANS

Materials

Empty cocoa cans or 12-oz. frozen orange juice cans;
Srpay paint in chosen color, or wallpaper remnants to cover cans;
Tacky glue;
Suitable pictures to decorate cans; used postage stamps make a very interesting collage;
Tapes, braids, rickrack or lace for trims;
Scissors;
Clear acrylic spray.

To Do Ahead—Director or Volunteers

If you are spraying the cans instead of covering them with wallpaper remnants, do this ahead.

Directions

1. If not spraying cans, cover with a pretty, but plain, wallpaper pattern, cut to a size to fold back over the top edge of the can about ½ inch.
2. Choose a suitable picture such as flowers, butterflies, fruits, a scene, faces, or postage stamps. Glue the picture on side or sides; postage stamps can be used to cover the entire can. Add any trims around the top or elsewhere and then spray with clear acrylic spray (see Figure 6-4).

6-4 Pencil Holders

Use or Display

These make lovely gifts or can be used in residents' rooms for decorations or holders for small items. They also make nice gifts to give staff.

Therapeutic Value

Ideas and creativity—choosing colors and wallpaper patterns and deciding on which pictures and trims to use for decorating one's cans can be quite creative;
Physical stimulation—use of arm and hand muscles, good eye-hand coordination;
Social value—conversation; give and take of ideas; cooperation with others;
Self-worth—creating something that can be used by others and can be given as a gift builds self-esteem.

SPICE CONTAINERS FROM SMALL MATCHING JARS

Materials

Small matching jars such as Wyler's beef or chicken broth cubes or the larger size baby food containers;
Stick-on letters in small sizes;
Small pictures of spices or spice leaves to decorate the jars (check plant catalogues or buy small decals);
White glue;
Scissors;
Small stick-on letters for names; Suggested spice names (short ones): cumin, basil, cloves, dill, sage, thyme, nutmeg, etc.

To Do Ahead—Director or Volunteers

Ask friends to save the jars until you have enough for a set of four for each worker. Buy decals or use magazines and catalogues for pictures.

Directions

1. Residents cut out the pictures. Center the small pictures of leaves or plants on one side of the jar and glue in place.
2. Arrange letters in a pleasing arrangement on opposite side of jar; stick them on at an angle or on the diagonal. See Figure 6-5 for ideas.

Use or Display

These make lovely gifts for a family member; several can be placed in a pretty box and wrapped as a gift.

6-5 Spice Jars

Therapeutic Value

Ideas and creativity—deciding on the spice, pictures, and colors each worker wants and determining where to place them on the jar involves some creativity;

Physical stimulation—work with the hands, arms, and fingers is good exercise to keep muscles more flexible;

Social value—visitation; conversation; cooperation with others;

Self-worth—creating a gift to give to a family member is a great booster of self-esteem.

COASTERS

Materials

Discarded rings from wide-mouth Mason jars;

Rounds of ⅛-inch thick cork. These should be 3⅜ inches in diameter, or a fraction smaller, so they will fit in the ring. Cork rounds ordered from a craft supply house will probably be 3¾ in size but can easily be trimmed with scissors;

Acrylic paint;

Paint brushes;

Stick-on decals;

Tacky glue;

Scissors;

Clear acrylic finish or spray to protect and make waterproof.

To Do Ahead—Director or Volunteers

If you are not able to buy the cork already cut to size, draw circles 3⅜ inches in diameter on a ⅛-inch thick sheet of cork; cut rounds carefully with a craft knife.

Directions

1. Paint jar rings desired color and let dry.
2. Place decals, pictures, or designs desired in the center of the cork round. Stick-on decals do not require glue, but other small pictures should be glued to the cork.

3. Spray or brush the top of the decorated cork round with clear acrylic so it will not absorb moisture.
4. Run a bead of glue around the inside of the jar ring and fit the cork round into the ring, pressing down well. Leave to dry.

Use or Display

These make fine gifts for friends or family, and can be offered to visitors to the home when drinks are served. They can also be sold at craft fairs.

Therapeutic Value

Ideas and creativity—choosing designs, pictures, or decals to use on the jar rings. Always let the workers make all the choices they are able to make;
Physical stimulation—using arm, hand and fingers to put the jar ring coaster together;
Social value—conversation; cooperation; helping others;
Self-worth—making gifts for family or friends builds self-esteem. Sharing is always important to the elderly.

EASTER OR MAY DAY BASKETS FROM DISCARDED BERRY BASKETS

Materials

Ribbons, bias tape, laces, braids and other trims. None should be over ½ inch wide.
Art paper or felt for flowers, or artificial flowers;
Twelve-inch chenille stems;
Tacky glue;
Shredded artificial grass for Easter baskets;
Twelve inches of 18-gauge wire for handles (unless you are using the chenille stems);
Scissors.

To Do Ahead—Director or Volunteers

For Easter baskets, cut out small flowers and leaves in various colors (if not using artificial flowers).

Directions

1. Make flowers and leaves from art paper or felt; glue them on the sides of basket; or cover sides with only ribbons and other trims.
2. Run ribbon or bias tape in and out through holes at the top of basket; tie ends in a bow.
3. Rickrack or other trim material such as lace, braid, or ribbon may be run through holes at bottom of basket (See Figure 6-6).
4. Fill basket about half full of artificial grass.

5. For a handle, twist two pieces of chenille stem together and attach to basket at sides by bending each end and bringing it up through side of basket, twisting to hold.

6. Wrap handle with ribbon or bias tape and tie a bow at each side of basket where handle joins.

7. Add enough glue to hold all trims in place.

8. Fill the baskets with candy eggs or hand-decorated eggs made by the residents. If making a May Day basket, use ribbons around top to add a small paper doily nosegay (See Part II).

6-6 Decorated Berry Basket

Use or Display

Easter baskets filled with candy eggs make wonderful gifts for children or for an Easter egg hunt. May baskets may be hung on each door or placed in each room on the first of May and could contain a small gift or a nosegay.

Therapeutic Value

Ideas and creativity—most residents will use their own ideas about which decorations to use on their basket; self-expression;

Physical stimulation—good arm, hand, and finger movement; eye-hand coordination;

Social value—conversation about Easter and May Day; cooperation; helping others;

Sense of self-worth—sharing, contribution to the children of the community and to the nursing home. Such contributions build self-confidence;

Memory orientation—remembering and talking about past Easters and May Days;

Reality orientation—recognizing the season.

COLORFUL BATH DECORATION FROM BAR SOAP

Materials

Bars of oval shaped soaps in various colors; white and green are good for Christmas, white and pink for Valentine's Day, blue with gold trim on white for Hanukkah or any other time of the year;

Twelve inches of rickrack; small ribbon or gold trim (no more than ½ inch wide);

One 3-inch artificial flower or 2 very small flowers and 4 or 5 artificial leaves;

Twelve tiny pearl beads or other beads;

Short sewing pins;

Scissors.

To Do Ahead—Director and Volunteers

Buy bar soaps and have decorative materials at hand.

Directions

1. Mark a 1½-inch square on the bottom center of soap.
2. Put two pearls each on four pins and insert them at a 45 degree angle at each of the four corners of the marked square. Because these will form the legs, turn soap over and adjust pins until legs are level (see Figure 6-7).
3. Circle the soap with the chosen trims, securing them with 4 beaded pins, one on each of the two sides and one on each of the two ends.
4. Pin leaves first and then flowers in a pleasing arrangement on top of soap, making sure they are all securely anchored. If the soap is to be used for scenting a clothes drawer, the leg pins should be omitted. Design the trims in a color to go with the season.

Use or Display

To use on bathroom counter or as a sweet-smelling scent for lingerie drawer. These also make appreciated Christmas gifts and can be sold in a craft fair.

Therapeutic Value

Ideas and creativity—letting residents choose their own materials to work makes the project more creative;

Physical stimulation—good for arm, hand, and finger muscles; eye-hand coordination;

Social value—working together; conversation and visitation; giving help to those who are less skilled;

Self-worth—creating something beautiful to be used in one's room or to give as a gift, or sell at a fair can add to one's self-esteem;

Sensory stimulation—stimulates the sense of smell.

6-7 Decorated Soaps

PASTA DECORATIONS

PASTA-DECORATED CHRISTMAS TREES

Materials

Empty yarn cones—one for each worker. These can be ordered from any good craft house for about $1.25 a dozen;
A variety of pasta in all forms. Colors are now available;
Tacky glue;
Heavy cardboard rings or paper towel tubes (if a base is desired);
Spray paint in chosen color.

To Do Ahead—Director or Volunteers

Put the different kinds of pasta in muffin tins or other small containers to keep the varieties separated. Spray paint the base cones and let dry.

Directions

1. Work out a pleasing pattern of pasta for the tree before gluing.
2. Glue on pasta until the entire cone is covered. (Figure 6-8) Put glue on only a small part of the cone at a time.
3. Glue on the ring base if one is desired. The tree can be used almost as effectively without the base and is much easier for less skilled participants to handle.
4. Spray paint the entire tree; decorate with star or butterfly at the top; glue a few small berries and holly leaves or tiny ornaments to the tree at strategic locations.

Variations

These trees are eye-catching in white with red and green decorations or can be painted blue and decorated with gold decorations, or sprayed gold and decorated with red or blue.

Use or Display

A group of three cones makes a beautiful table decoration as well as one cone tree used in the center of a smaller table.

Therapeutic Value

Ideas and creativity—working out designs with help and deciding on color desired is an expression of self;
Physical stimulation—good eye-hand coordination; use of arms, hands, and fingers;
Social value—conversation; cooperation with others; visitation;

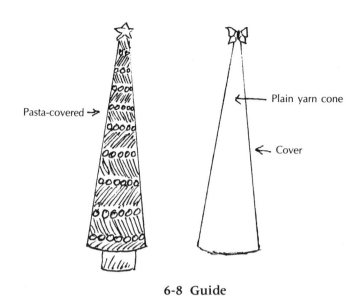

Pasta-covered →

— Plain yarn cone

← Cover

6-8 Guide

Self-worth—sharing one's creations with the nursing center and the community; making the
   center more beautiful for Christmas;

Reality orientation—remembering the season;

Memory orientation—remembering other Christmastimes and the decorations that were used for
   the tables.

PASTA AND SHELL JEWELRY

Materials

Pasta of various sizes and shapes (with a hole through it so it can be strung). Pasta shells can also
   be used if drilled with a very small drill;

Small beads to go between the pasta pieces;

Acrylic paint;

Brushes for painting;

Corking, ribbon, or macrame cord for stringing pasta and beads;

Tacky glue;

Long round pointed needles used for stringing;

Cardboard or thin clay backing for pasta pins or earrings;

Clear acrylic spray;

Scissors.

To Do Ahead—Director or Volunteers

Sort the pasta and put into muffin tins or small containers. Put the different colored beads in small
containers to keep them separate.

Directions

1. If you want the necklace or other jewelry to be colored, paint the pasta first by holding each piece on the point of a pencil and brushing on the paint; let dry. Pasta can be left its natural color and colored beads strung between the pasta pieces (Figure 6-9).
2. String the chosen pieces and beads on cord or a thin leather strip, being sure to have it long enough to tie at the back of the neck. Measure carefully before cutting.
3. When stringing is finished, spray the entire necklace or other jewelry with clear acrylic spray. This gives gloss and protects it.
4. If a pin or earrings have been made, the pasta must be glued to a jewelry finding (a pin backing for the pin and clips or posts for the earrings).

Variations

Small shells of various kinds may also be drilled with a small drill and strung on cord or ribbon to make a lovely necklace. Sand dollars (using only one on a pretty cord or ribbon) make handsome drop necklaces. They must be sprayed with *two* coats of clear acrylic spray to preserve them. Wait about two hours between each coating.

Use of Display

These can be worn by the residents, given as gifts, as prizes in bingo, or sold at a craft fair.

Therapeutic Value

Ideas and creativity—the workers can be very creative about jewelry because most of them like it. Listen to their ideas as much as possible and give guidance;

Physical stimulation—good use of hand and finger muscles; eye-hand coordination;

Social value—visitation and talking about preferred jewelry; cooperation with those who are less skilled;

Self-worth—this project can be a great source of pride. If the jewelry is well made enough to use as bingo prizes and give for gifts, it will greatly add to self-esteem.

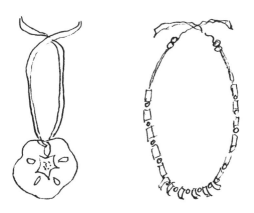

6-9 Shell and Pasta Jewelry

SHELL OR PASTA-COVERED JEWELRY BOX

Materials

Small wooden, plastic, tin, or heavy cardboard boxes (painted or covered with papier-mâché and then painted);
Packages of assorted small shells available from craft supply houses, or a variety of pasta shapes;
White or tacky glue;
Clear acrylic spray;
Paint brushes;
Water-based paint, thinned (peach, pink, yellow or lavender for the shells) or gold or silver spray paint.

To Do Ahead—Director, Volunteers or Residents

Sort shells or pasta into types and sizes; have boxes painted and dry.

Directions

1. Work out the design for the box before gluing anything down.
2. When design is satisfactory, glue shells or pasta down, applying glue heavily in one small space at a time so it will not dry out too quickly.
3. When the box is covered, wash with diluted pale color if desired. Gold or silver spray is beautiful for shells or pasta.
4. Spray with clear acrylic to protect the box, give gloss, and help to hold the shells in place (Figure 6-10).

Use or Display

Use in residents' rooms, to give as gifts, for bingo prizes, or to sell at a craft fair.

Therapeutic Value

Ideas and creativity—working out designs and choosing colors involve self-expression;
Physical stimulation—good eye-hand coordination; use of arm, hand, and fingers.
Social value—conversation; cooperation with others; helping others who are less skilled;
Self-worth—excellent for self-esteem if used for gifts, bingo prizes or to sell at craft fairs. The projects also make conversation pieces for use in seniors' rooms.

6-10 Pasta/Shell-Covered Box

TICK-TACK-TOE GAME

Materials

Plywood or chipboard, ⅛ inch thick, twelve inches square;
White spray paint;
Black permanent marker or black acrylic paint and small brush;
Ten clay pieces (for the board) made from modeling clay in a craft session; five painted red, five
  painted blue with acrylic paint.
Clear acrylic spray;
Ruler;
Pencil.

To Do Ahead—Director and Volunteers

Cut plywood or chipboard into 12-inch squares; spray paint white; let dry.

Directions

1. Divide the painted chipboard into nine 4-inch squares by carefully measuring with the ruler and marking off (Figure 6-11).
2. Mark the lines with a black permanent marker or paint with black acrylic paint with a very small brush.
3. Let dry thoroughly.
4. Use ten clay pieces or tokens made by the residents (five bright red and five bright blue). The pieces need to be at least 2 inches in diameter so they can easily be handled by the players. Spray board and pieces with clear acrylic spray.

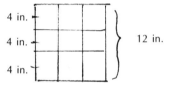

6-11 Guide: Tick-Tack-Toe

Use or Display

For use of seniors or to give as a gift to a child. This is a very old game, but still fun. The two players may draw to see who moves first. The first player places one of the red tokens in any square he or she chooses. The second player (with all blue tokens) places his or her token in another square. The object of the game is to place all three of one's tokens in a straight line, either vertical, horizontal or diagonal, while keeping the opposite player from getting his tokens in a line. The first player to get three tokens in a line wins the game.

Therapeutic Value

Physical stimulation—only arms and hand use involved in playing the game; and making board.
Social value—great social value involved in the interaction of two players and their ability to give and take;
Self-worth—playing and winning a game can give feelings of accomplishment and self-esteem; making one's own game adds to these feelings.

7

Table, Party, and Christmas Decorations

PARTY THEMES

People everywhere love a party and nursing home residents are certainly no exception. These occasions provide an opportunity for them to see friends and people from the community, to enjoy special refreshments and original table decorations. Many of the centerpiece designs have special themes and most can be created, at least partially, in the weekly craft sessions. Simple designs for paper flowers are included in Part II.

The patterns for Christmas decorations are quite extensive: (this is a very important festive occasion for many residents). Included are special designs for general decoration, table centerpieces, the tree, the residents' rooms, and the bulletin board.

"Do you Remember?" Questions to Stimulate Reality and Memory Orientation

- Do you remember the kind of Christmas you knew as a child?
- What kinds of decorations were used about the house and on the tree?
- Where did you get your tree (if you had one)?
- What did you receive for Christmas?
- What did your children receive?
- What were your family's Christmas customs?
- Do you remember parties you enjoyed?
- What kinds of parties were they?
- Working parties?
- Wedding parties?
- Dances?
- Family get-togethers?
- What did you enjoy most?
- What did you have for refreshment?

THE DECORATIONS

Party decorations should be bright and colorful and residents should have a part in the creation of them. Food served needs to be different from the same old party fare of punch, cookies and cake. Plan the menu to fit the theme of the party and be creative.

110

HAWAIIAN LUAU

The women can wear flowers in their hair, leis should be made for the men. Flowered straight dresses and shell necklaces look festive and native to the islands. Everyone should wear bright colors. The tables can be decorated with paper flowers made by the residents, mixed with shells, on woven mats or small fishnets. Large fishnets with cork floats and pieces of driftwood can be used to decorate the room. Use many, many flowers.

The food served might be sweet and sour chicken, barbequed ribs, candied yams or baked potatoes, banana nut bread, and assorted fresh fruits. Find a menu that fits the theme.

For entertainment play Hawaiian music and show a film on Hawaii. Perhaps someone in the community has slides from the islands that they would be willing to show.

It might be fun to learn some Hawaiian words: *Kāne*— man; *wăhine*— woman; *ono*— delicious; *luau*— feast; *Tutu*— grandma; *Tutu Kāne*— grandpa; *wiki-wiki*— hurry up; *mahalo*— thank you; and *aloha*— hello, goodbye, or I love you.

MEXICAN THEME PARTY

The women can wear bright skirts or dresses, fancy embroidered blouses, large earrings and other jewelry—anything that says Mexico. Men can wear large Mexican straw hats if available or brightly colored bandanas at neck. The tables can be decorated with handmade paper flowers or papier-mâché fruits on straw mats or baskets. The room might be decorated with Eyes of God, pinatas, or in the colors of the Mexican flag—red, green and white. Large Mexican hats also make effective decorations. The table covers should be bright and gay. Ladies might wear flowers in their hair; the men might wear boutonnieres. The staff should also be dressed Mexican style.

The food served could be a mild Mexican meal (many residents say they would love some tamales). Try to vary the refreshments from the meals they ordinarily have.

For entertainment provide Mexican music and a slide program on the beauty of Mexico.

ITALIAN THEME PARTY

The staff and seniors can wear peasant costumes—bright full skirts, fancy white blouses, chunky jewelry, wide sashes, etc.

The tables might be decorated with red and white checked tablecloths, with candles in wine bottles (ahead of time burn candles that drip, so the wax can run down the sides of the bottles). Papier-mâché fruits or grapes can also be used on the tables in baskets.

The food served could be various kinds of pizza or spaghetti and meat balls, a green salad, Italian bread, a non-alcoholic drink and ice cream or fresh fruits and cheeses.

Entertainment could include a film or slides focusing on the wonderful art of Italy or the beauty of the charming old hillside villages.

ORIENTAL THEME PARTY

The theme of the party might be the figures used to indicate the Chinese new year. 1990 is the year of the horse, 1991, the year of the ram, 1992, the year of the monkey. Residents might make

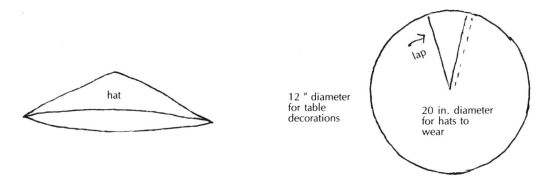

7-1 Coolie hat

coolie hats for everyone taking part in the party. To make hats, draw large circles—20-inch diameter—on wallpaper-covered cardboard. Cut out the circles; make a slit from the edge to the center; overlap edges to form hat; and glue in place. Staple if needed to help hold hat together. Reds, deep reds, rich blues and gold are the colors to use (Figure 7-1).

The tables can be decorated with the appropriate animal of the Chinese year. Extra coolie hats and wind chimes made by the residents can be used for room decoration.

Serve sweet and sour chicken, stir-fry pork and rice, fruit, and fortune cookies. Tea is the appropriate drink.

For entertainment provide Oriental music and slides of China. Many times friends in the community who have visited China will have slide shows to share.

CLOWN AND CIRCUS PARTY

August 1–7 is National Clown Week, so that month is a good time to have a circus party. The staff might dress in clown costumes and wear clown make-up. The residents enjoy the fun of this. The tables could be decorated with white tablecloths with big red dots painted on. (Use old white sheets and let the residents paint the dots, using a template.) On each table use helium balloons attached to something heavy to hold them down. Use all bright colors or use only red and white to complement the tablecloths.

Serve hot dogs, peanuts, popcorn, and lots of pop. The room can be decorated with balloons, clowns (see patterns in Part VIII) and circus animals. The film "Dumbo" or other circus film might be shown.

DECORATIONS FOR OCTOBER TABLES

Let the residents decorate pumpkins for each table. Put hair on the pumpkins by using wigs, false hair, or finely shredded crepe paper. Cut out eyes or draw them with markers. Fit the heads with eyeglasses, hats, pipes. Paint lips red for female pumpkins and with marker make big eyes and long eyelashes. This is a place for imagination—you can think of many more ways to dress a pumpkin. If you have plastic pumpkins with a hole cut in the top, you might fill them with strawflowers to use as table decorations. The room can be decorated with lots of paper autumn leaves made by the residents and placed in baskets or containers made in craft sessions.

Serve pumpkin pie with whipped topping and coffee.

October is Popcorn Poppin' month so you might have a popcorn party with a variety of popcorn flavors for testing. Carmel corn is delicious, just be careful that it is not too sticky for those who have false teeth.

The craft group might make popcorn florals from any left over popcorn.

OTHER CELEBRATIONS

National Ice Cream Week is July 10–16; this is a fine time for a yearly ice cream party. The bulletin board might have ice cream cone decorations at that time.

A party can be planned to celebrate almost any ethnic group by following the ideas above and planning decorations, apparel, food, and entertainment appropriate to the theme.

CHRISTMAS DECORATIONS

WREATHS FOR CHRISTMAS OR OTHER HOLIDAYS

Materials

Small wreaths—straw or grapevine;
Ribbon in a color to suit the season, ½ inch wide;
White tacky glue;
Appropriate decorations: small Christmas ornaments for Christmas wreath, bits of holly and berries, tiny wrapped packages; colored leaves and acorns or other seed pods for autumn; small birds, butterflies, or flowers for spring or May Day; pink or red ribbons, lace, and hearts for Valentine wreaths;
Soft florist's wire;
Wire cutter

To Do Ahead—Director, Volunteers, and Residents

Make the wreaths or buy them, one for each resident. Residents can cut ribbons to proper length using a sample to cut by.

Directions

1. Give each worker a wreath. Let workers choose the color of ribbon and the decorations that they would like to have on their wreath.
2. Have the workers wrap the ribbon around the wreath in a diagonal fashion (Figure 7-2).
3. Cut the ends of the ribbon and glue them together.
4. Glue or tie the decorations on the wreath in an artistic design, or hang one flat ornament in the center. (7-2).

7-2 Guide for Fancy Wreaths

5. Allow the glue to dry. Tie a ribbon bow for the top of the wreath, attaching it with soft wire and at the same time making a loop on the back of the wreath for hanging.

Use or Display

Hang wreaths beside each door in the halls or hang in seniors' rooms. Some wreaths may be made for other doors in the center so each door will be decorated.

Variations

Wreaths may be used for any season of the year by changing the decorations and the color of the ribbons.

Therapeutic Value

Ideas and creativity—this exercise can be very creative for the participants, choosing colors and types of decorations;

Physical stimulation—use of arm and finger muscles; hand-eye coordination;

Social value—cooperation with others in making the wreaths, helping those less skilled with the work, conversation; and visiting;

Sense of self-worth—sharing, contribution to the center as a whole. Making wreaths to be used on the doors of those who are unable to participate gives one a sense of self-esteem.

CHRISTMAS DECORATIONS—PLACEMATS

Materials

Contact paper in red, green, white, and clear;
Lightweight cardboard;
Old Christmas cards;
White glue;
Scissors.

To Do Ahead—Director and Volunteers

Cut the cardboard and colored contact paper to a 12 × 15-inch rectangle or a circle 15 inches in diameter. Cut clear contact paper ½ inch larger for covering mats.

Directions

1. Place colored contact paper on the cardboard for a more stable base. Show residents how to place it evenly along the sides and top *before* pressing down.
2. Cut desired pictures from cards (let workers choose) and place in a pleasing arrangement on the base mat.
3. When the design looks right, glue the cutouts in place.
4. Take cut piece of clear contact paper and carefully fit it over the mat, turning the extra ½ inch to the back side and pressing down carefully so it adheres. This protects the mat and it can be wiped clean.
5. Put the worker's name on the back of the mat for mealtime use.

Variation

White contact paper and old valentines cut up, glued on and covered with clear contact paper can be used for Valentine's Day parties. The mats could be made for any season.

Use or Display

These mats are nice to use on the tables—especially for the residents who have designed and made them. Some extras can be made for those who do not participate in the craft program.

Therapeutic Value

Ideas and creativity—this is a very creative and simple activity;
Participants choose their own pictures and arrange them to their own liking;
Physical stimulation—Good use of hand and fingers and hand-eye coordination;
Social value—conversation; cooperation; helping those who are less skilled;
Sense of self-worth—sharing; making mats for those who are not able to make them for themselves; contributing to the beauty of the tables in the center.

PICTURE ORNAMENTS FOR CHRISTMAS TREE

Materials

Plastic lids from ½-pound margarine tubs or 1-pound coffee cans.
    Have one for each participant whose picture will be used on the home Christmas tree. This should include all seniors if possible;
Narrow ribbon in red or gold for hangers;
Tacky glue;
Scissors;
Photos of residents of nursing home, close-ups preferred;
Paper punch;
Five or six yards of 1-inch ribbon for bows on tree;
Spray paint in gold or red.

7-3 Picture Ornaments

To Do Ahead—Director and Volunteers

Take good close-up photos of seniors; have them ready for the craft session. Spray paint the lids in the chosen color (or use two colors); cut residents' photos in circular shapes in a size to fit the lids with about ½ inch of lid showing around the edge.

Directions

1. Glue the cut-out pictures to the exact center of the painted lids.
2. Punch a small hole in the top of the lid with a paper punch.
3. Thread the ribbon through the hole and tie in a small bow for hanging on the tree (Figure 7-3).
4. Tie the one-inch ribbon in bows to place on the tree with the photographs. Add any other decorations which seem to fit the color scheme, such as gold tinsel.

Use or Display

These are nice used on a medium-sized tree to share with family and friends.

Therapeutic Value

Ideas and creativity—not a great deal of creativity involved, but residents love seeing their pictures on the tree;

Physical stimulation—some hand-eye coordination involved in placement of the photos and gluing them down;

Social value—a great deal of social value, making hangers for those unable to do it for themselves;

Sense of self-worth—sharing is important contribution to the nursing center; sharing with family and friends at Christmas.

CANDY CANE SLEIGH

Materials

Two 7-inch candy canes for each worker (try to find straight ones);
Cardboard box for each sleigh, about 5½ inches long and 2½ inches wide (or find boxes and fit the canes to the box);

Red velvet ribbon, about 16 inches long, or red felt cut to the same size. Ribbon or felt should be
  wide enough to cover the side of the box;
Red tissue paper for inside the box;
Trims, white lace, sequins, gold braids, rickrack or anything you have available for decoration;
White tacky glue;
Scissors;
Wrapped candy to fill sleigh.

To Do Ahead—Director and Volunteers

Have boxes ready.

Directions

1. Glue wide, straight edge of ribbon or felt to the outside edge of the box. Notch the bottom edge of the ribbon so that the notches are over the corners of the box. Fold down and glue folded edges to the inside rim of the box.
2. Glue white lace and other decorative items on box. When dry, turn box upside down.
3. Leave peppermint sticks in their wrapping, but cut off any excess paper at curved end of canes so they will fit tightly against the box when glued.
4. Put two lines of glue across bottom of box ¼ inch in from each side and put glue on the tip of the curved end of cane.
5. Press the long arms of canes on the glue strips and the curved ends against the front of box. Hold a few minutes until glue is set.
6. Leave box turned down until thoroughly dry. Then turn up. Stuff bottom of box with crushed tissue paper and fill with wrapped Christmas candy (Figure 7-4).

Use or Display

The sleighs can be used as gifts or room decorations, or be displayed at an art show.

Therapeutic Value

Ideas and creativity—workers choose their own decorations for the sleigh they are making. This
  can be quite creative;
Physical stimulation—use of hand, finger, and arm muscles, hand-eye coordination;
Social value—conversation; visiting; sharing; contribution to the Christmas feeling of the home;
Sense of self-worth—satisfaction of creating something that can be used to decorate the rooms or
  can be given as a gift to family and friends.
Reality orientation—A reminder that Christmas is close at hand.

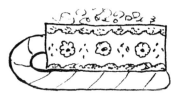

7-4 Candy Cane Sleigh

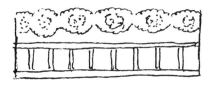

CANDY CANE DECORATIONS

Materials

Large size candy canes—6 to 7 inches long;
Twelve inches of 2 inch wide insertion lace with eyelets large
   enough to slip canes through. Check fabric outlets (Figure
   7-5);
Twelve to fourteen inches of red ribbon for bow, ½ inch
   wide;
Small cluster of dried or artificial flowers, or holly and berries;
Scissors.

7-5 2 Inch Wide Insertion Lace

To Do Ahead—Director or Volunteers

Have ready the insertion lace and canes on the worktable.

Directions

1. Slip insertion lace onto cane, trimming even at the end.
2. Tie a red bow with flower or berry cluster and place just below the curve
   in the cane (Figure 7-6).
3. Make as many as needed for tree decorations.

7-6 Candy Cane
Decorations

Use or Display

These decorations can be used on Christmas tree, in residents' rooms, as gifts, or display in an art
show.

Therapeutic Value

Ideas and creativity—not a great deal of creative ideas—only choosing the spray to be tied on the
   cane;
Physical stimulation—hand-eye coordination; finger and hand muscle use;
Social value—cooperation and sharing; helping others;
Sense of self-worth—ability to make something to decorate the tree or to give as a gift, making the
   nursing center look more beautiful.

HANGING FOAM CHRISTMAS BALL

Materials

One 4-inch plastic foam ball for each worker (or if only a few balls are wanted for
   decoration, let several people work on one ball;
Sprigs of boxwood, holly, or evergreens, real or artificial, enough to cover the ball closely;
Two yards of ½ inch wide red ribbon to tie small bows on hairpins, to stick among the greenery;
Small wire hairpins or other thin wire;

Two small redbirds, two small red apples, or two large pine cones (or anything else you like to decorate the top of the ball);

One and a half yards of 1½ inch wide red ribbon for hanging and for the flat bow at top of hanging ball.

To Do Ahead

Cut short the stems of boxwood or evergreen sprigs. Some of the residents might enjoy going along. Or provide artificial sprigs if you want the balls to last over a long period of time.

Directions

1. Strip lower leaves from sprigs if using fresh greens and stick them into the plastic ball very close together.
2. When ball is covered, tie small red ribbon bows onto wire hairpin or other wire and stick them among the greens. Red berries on wire are also very attractive.
3. Attach the two small birds, cones, fruit, or poinsettias into the top of the ball. An angel (or two small angels) could also be used, or bells could be hung from the bottom of the ball. (Figure 7-7)
4. Tie a flat bow with ⅓ of the larger ribbon and use the remainder to hang the ball, doubling it and attaching it to the ball with a hairpin.

Use or Display

These decorations can be hung at any spot in the nursing center at Christmas, given as a gift to family, or displayed at an art show.

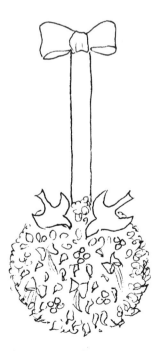

7-7 Hanging Christmas Ball

Therapeutic Value

Ideas and creativity—this project allows for a great deal of creativity in choosing the materials to go on the hanging ball;

Physical stimulation—arm and hand muscle use, plus the walk to gather materials;

Social value—conversation; visiting as the work progresses; cooperation with and helping others;

Sense of self-worth—a sharing experience; contribution to the nursing center as a whole; gift giving;

Memory orientation—a reminder of the nearness of Christmas.

ADVENT CALENDARS

ADVENT CALENDER—STREET SCENE

Materials

Two large poster boards, one for backing and one for front;

Art paper for house cutouts (unless you prefer to paint them);

Acrylic paint and brushes—colors in soft blues, browns, rose, burgundy, and gold;

Craft knife for cutting openings (to be used only by director);

Tacky glue;

Gold paint or marker;

Scissors; Pencil

Old Christmas cards

To Do Ahead—Director or Volunteers

Trace and enlarge the drawing (Figure 7-8) with a pantograph 4 or 5 times, less if you want a smaller calendar. You can also use a picture of any interesting group of buildings with *many* doors and windows. You will need 25 openings.

Directions

1. Cut out building shapes from art paper and glue on the top poster board. Or paint the building shapes on the top board in soft shades of colors listed above.
2. Cut out the openings with a craft knife (director or volunteers). They can then be folded back to open.
3. Lay the top piece of poster board with the cut-out openings over the bottom piece; with a pencil, on the bottom poster board mark carefully around the openings.
4. Lift off the top piece; from old Christmas cards cut pictures to fit openings; glue them into the spaces outlined. Save the large door space in center of calendar for a picture of the Nativity.
5. When all pictures are glued on the bottom half, glue the top half of the board over it. Starting on December 1, open a window each day until Christmas, saving the large door with the Nativity until the 25th.

7-8 Drawing for Advent Calendar—Buildings

Use or Display

If you are using the calendar just as a Christmas decoration, it can be used anywhere in the nursing center. If you use it as a Christmas bulletin board, you can cut the small packages or stars illustrated in Part VIII for an activity calendar. The residents love opening the windows and doors.

Therapeutic Value

Ideas and creativity—choosing the pictures they want to show in the openings is a form of self-expression;
Physical stimulation—hand-eye coordination; use of hands and fingers;
Social value—visiting; conversation; cooperation;
Sense of self-worth—sharing memories with each other; contributing to the holiday beauty of the nursing center; satisfaction of creating something everyone can enjoy;
Memory orientation—remembering past Christmases.

ADVENT CALENDAR—CHRISTMAS TREE

Materials

Green poster board or green felt for tree, brown for tree holder;
Bright red art paper for cards to hang on tree;
Gold cord or ¼-inch ribbon to tie on cards;
Gold glitter or gold foil paper for numbers and for star at top of tree;
Old Christmas cards;
Scissors;
Tacky glue;
Stapler to attach cards to tree;
Paper punch

To Do Ahead—Director and Volunteers

Trace and enlarge the drawing (Figure 7-9) 6 or 7 times larger on the pantograph, depending on the size of the space you have. Seven times makes a tree about 31½ inches high.

Directions

1. Cut tree out of green poster board or green felt and cut the tree base holder from brown poster board or felt.
2. Cut 5 × 6-inch rectangles from the bright red art paper and fold in the center to make a card 2½ × 3 inches, folded.
3. Write the numbers with glue and sprinkle with glitter, or cut numbers out of gold foil paper and glue on the cards.
4. Cut Christmas motifs or scenes from the old cards and glue a picture inside each card.
5. The cards are tied on the sides with gold ribbon or cord bow (Figure 7-10). Punch holes 1 inch apart and slightly in from folded edge of card, if tying, or glue. The card can then be stapled to the tree.

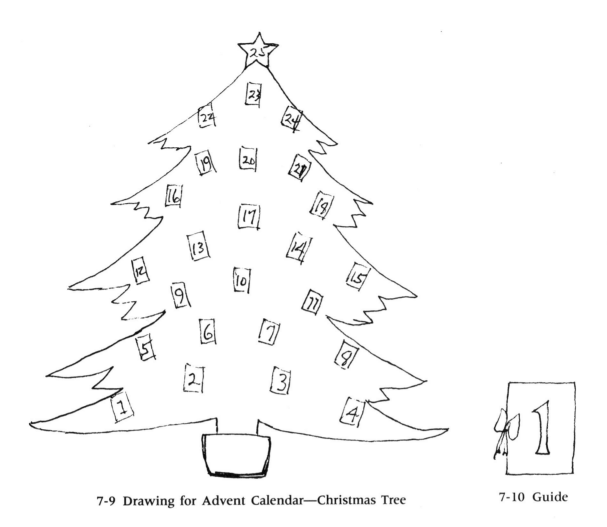

7-9 Drawing for Advent Calendar—Christmas Tree   **7-10 Guide**

6. Open one card a day until the 25th of December. Then add the gold star to the top for Christmas Day. Start a lovely custom.

Use or Display

Use as an Advent calendar anywhere in the nursing center or use as a December bulletin board. If using as a bulletin board, cut stars to use for the activity calendar.

Therapeutic Value

Ideas and creativity—creativity is involved in choosing the pictures for the cards. Let workers use their own ideas.
Physical stimulation—hand-eye coordination; muscle use for fingers and hands;
Social value—visiting and conversation; cooperation with others; helping those who are less skilled to make their own cards for the tree;
Sense of self-worth—sharing the calendar with the nursing home and the community; satisfaction of creating a lovely Christmas decoration and adding to the holiday spirit;
Reality orientation—recognizing the season of the year.

8

Bulletin Boards and Activity Calendars

BULLETIN BOARDS AND ACTIVITY CALENDARS

Many residents of nursing homes and day care centers lose track of the days, months, and seasons of the year. Seasonal decorations and monthly bulletin boards, with a day by day calendar of events, seem to help them relate to the passing of time and keep a sense of reality. Men are sometimes forgotten in planning bulletin boards, but you will find a number of the suggested ideas appeal to men. Most of the ideas are suited to both sexes, with a few designed primarily for women.

The bulletin boards also stimulate recollections. One of the most valuable assets of the elderly is memory. They may not remember too much of the present but they recall a great deal of information about the past. This is not only beneficial to them for keeping their minds active, but can be of value to others who need to know something of the mores, views, and experiences of the past in order to understand their own place in history.

If you have a large flat box in which to store your bulletin board materials when they are taken down, they can be used in different combinations again and again. Residents change and many do not remember a board for more than a year. Many of the ideas can be used at times of the year other than the months suggested; so the materials are worth storing and keeping, at least for a period of time.

Bulletin Board Ideas

Bulletin boards are to keep residents aware of days and months, but can also be used to alert them to what is happening in their own community and those themes can be used to decorate the bulletin board for the month.

Listed below are some of the names of fairs, festivals, fests, contests, etc.

Shell fairs (along coastal regions) use some of the shell designs
Azalea trails or festivals—in certain parts of the country
Dogwood festivals—in many places around the country
Mountain laurel festival
Magnolia festival
Yellow daisy festival
Festival of roses
Peanut festival
Apple festival

Strawberry festival
Peach festival
Pecan festival
Cotton festival
Various wild flower festivals
Cranberry festival
Seafood festivals
Waterfowl festival
Buccaneer days
Sailboat races
Autumn leaves festival
Music festival
Bluegrass festival
Old fiddler's contest
Jazz festival
Indian fairs
Rodeos
Kite festivals
Vintage car fest
Mardi Gras days
Fiestas

These are only a few, but you will know what events take place in your part of the country and can suit your bulletin board to the event.

Many of the pictures you will need can be found in this book, others will be available locally. If you need to copy a design, use your pantograph and design your bulletin board accordingly. By keeping these local happenings in mind and using them to provide illustrations for your bulletin boards, you not only help yourself by providing a theme, but help the residents to relate to what goes on in their community.

IDEAS FOR BULLETIN BOARDS—LOCAL FESTIVALS, FAIRS, AND JUBILEES

To illustrate how to use festivals in planning a bulletin board, we will plan for five festivals within a 30 mile radius of our area.

Strawberry Festival

For the main part of the bulletin board, use a picture of a large basket of strawberries with a few berries and leaves lying beside the basket. Use large strawberries for the activity calendar, making the strawberry for the day of the festival in a little different color or shape to call attention to the day.

Peanut Festival

For the main part of the bulletin board, use an enlargement of the "Mr. Peanut" design on any Planter's product. Use your pantograph to enlarge it to proper size. For the activity calendar, cut out peanut shapes in a tan-colored paper and mark with a few brown lines. During festival time, the craft group can make peanut necklaces by spraying peanuts with gold spray paint, punching small holes in one end (have someone drill them with a very small drill), and stringing them on a gold cord.

Watermelon Thump

In the bulletin board section, you will find a watermelon theme bulletin board. Simply use this for the month of the Thump.

Fiesta

This is a celebration with a Mexican flavor. A suggested theme for the fiesta poster is Eyes of God. Use the Eye weavings suggested in the bulletin board section. Mexican hats can be used for the calendar; brightly colored paper balloons could also be used.

Dogwood Festival

For the main board use an enlarged spray of dogwood; for the calendar, use dogwood blossoms with a few lines on them to indicate the flower.

If your bulletin board calendar is the ready-made type that you simply fill in, decorate it with some of the designs suggested in this section in order to tie it in with the bulletin board theme of the month.

BULLETIN BOARD IDEAS FOR THE TWELVE MONTHS OF THE YEAR

Bulletin Board Ideas for January or February

SNOWMEN

Materials

White poster board for bodies;
Glue and stapler for assembling;
Snowman I—red striped fabric for scarf (Figure 8-1);
Large black buttons for eyes and shirt front; smaller black buttons for mouth and shirt front;
Orange felt for nose; red felt for cap; blue felt for gloves;
Snowman II—hat from black art paper or felt (Figure 8-2);
Black marker to draw black eye and mouth, red marker for nose;
Red pompom for ear muff (or can be cut from cardboard, outlined with red marker);
Red bow for tie (Snowman II);
Holly sprig and berries for hat (optional);
Scissors;
Glue.

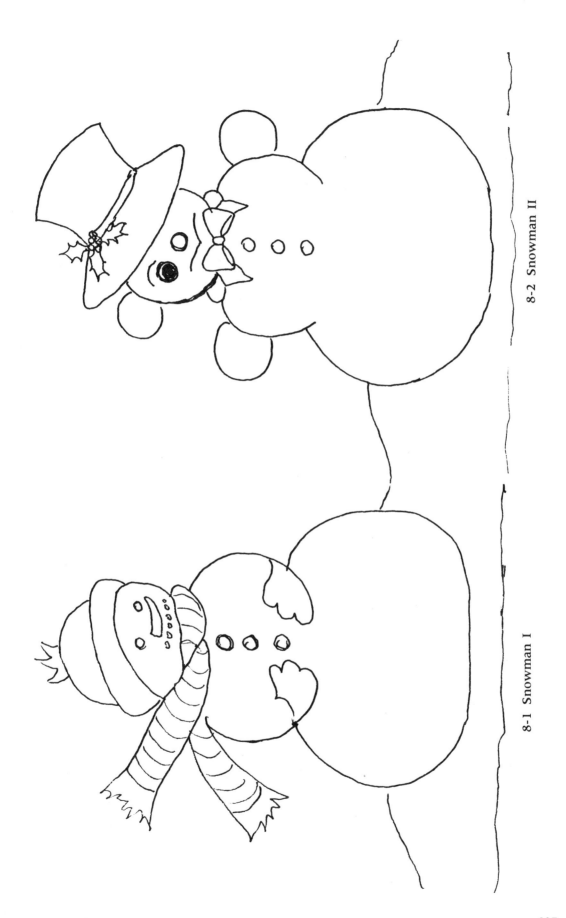

8-2 Snowman II

8-1 Snowman I

To Do Ahead

Trace pattern, enlarge with pantograph to 3 or 4 times original size or to a size suitable for your bulletin board. Measure carefully.

Directions

1. Trace enlarged pattern on poster board; cut out the bodies.
2. *Snowman I*—cut out felt cap, nose, gloves; glue on body, following pattern. Glue on button mouth and buttons on shirt front.
3. Make any necessary marks for eyes, mouth, and nose with marker and tie red striped fabric around neck. Staple the snowman to bulletin board.
4. *Snowman II*—Cut hat from black art paper or felt; glue onto body at the proper angle ("rakish").
5. Use black marker to draw eye and mouth, red marker for nose. Use small pompom or red marker for earmuff.
6. Glue black buttons down front; glue on red bow tie.
7. The snow bank for each snowman can be cut from white poster board; glue on a bit of artificial snow, if desired.

Calendar

Snowman II makes a wonderful calendar. Cut the shape from white construction paper and add details with markers.

PENGUINS

Materials

White poster board for bodies;
Glue;
Stapler;
Acrylic paint in black, grey, orange, and white;
Colored paper can be used instead of paint by cutting shapes and gluing on bodies in proper place;
White poster board or gift wrap paper for snow bank;
Small bit of artificial snow (if desired).

To Do Ahead

Trace patterns, enlarge with pantograph to three or four times the size given (or to a size suitable for your bulletin board). Measure carefully.

Directions

1. Trace enlarged pattern on poster board; cut out the body shapes.
2. Paint with acrylic paint where the colors are indicated on the patterns, or cut the parts from colored paper and glue on the bodies.

orange

grey   grey

black

white

8-3 Penguin I

3. Cut snowbank, add a little glue, and sprinkle with artificial snow. Staple penguins in place on bulletin board. See Figures 8-3 and 8-4.

Calendar

Use snowflake cutouts for the calendar (Figure 8-5). Doily edges may also be trimmed to resemble snowflakes and a shape cut from paper glued in the center for writing calendar notations. See Figure 8-5.

MUSICAL BOARD

Materials

White poster board for background;
Black ribbon ⅛ inches wide for the lines (amount depending on size of your bulletin board);
Glue;
Scissors;
Black construction or art paper, heavy foil for making notes;
Black marker for drawing staff lines.

To Do Ahead

Enlarge the outside shape with the pantograph and cut from white poster board. A four times enlargement is suggested (or a size suitable for your bulletin board space). Measure carefully.

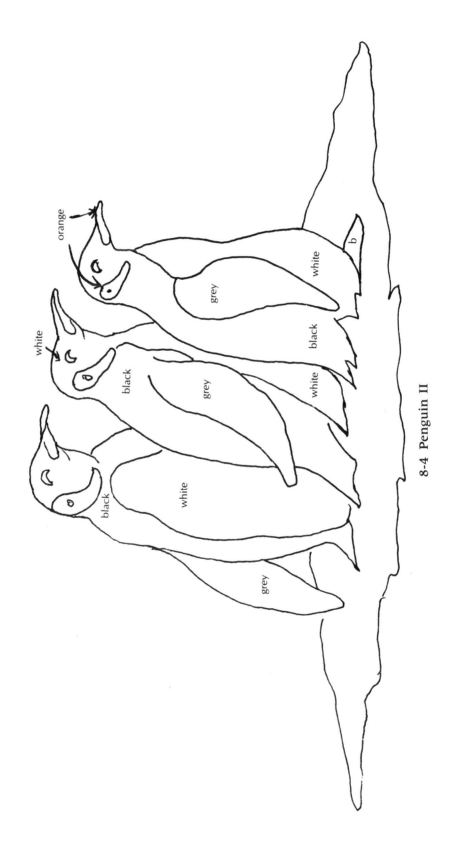

8-4 Penguin II

8-5 Snowflake Calendar

Directions

1. Mark the lines with the heavy black marker or glue on narrow black ribbon. Mark the staff lines and meter with black marker.
2. Cut the notes from black paper for the dark notes and silver for the white notes. Glue them in place and draw the stems on the notes with black marker; then add the words with marker (Figure 8-6).

Calendar

Bells make a wonderful calendar for this board, carrying out the music theme. For a January board, use poster board sprayed silver and write the calendar on the bells (Figure 8-7). Connect with a white or silver ribbon.

Variation

The enlarged bell shapes can also be used for a Christmas bulletin board. Cut them from gold-sprayed poster board and arrange on board as indicated on pattern. Make the calendar from the same gold board; glue on a small rectangle of bright red paper for writing the calendar notations; use red ribbon for joining the bells together for the calendar.

REDBIRDS IN THE SNOW

Materials

White and grey construction or art paper, or bright red art paper;
Acrylic paint, bright red, or orange and black;
White gift wrap paper;
Glue;
Brushes;
Scissors;
Artificial snow;
A few real sunflower seeds.

To Do Ahead

Trace the birds and post pattern (Figure 8-8) and enlarge with pantograph 2 or 3 times, depending on size of your bulletin board.

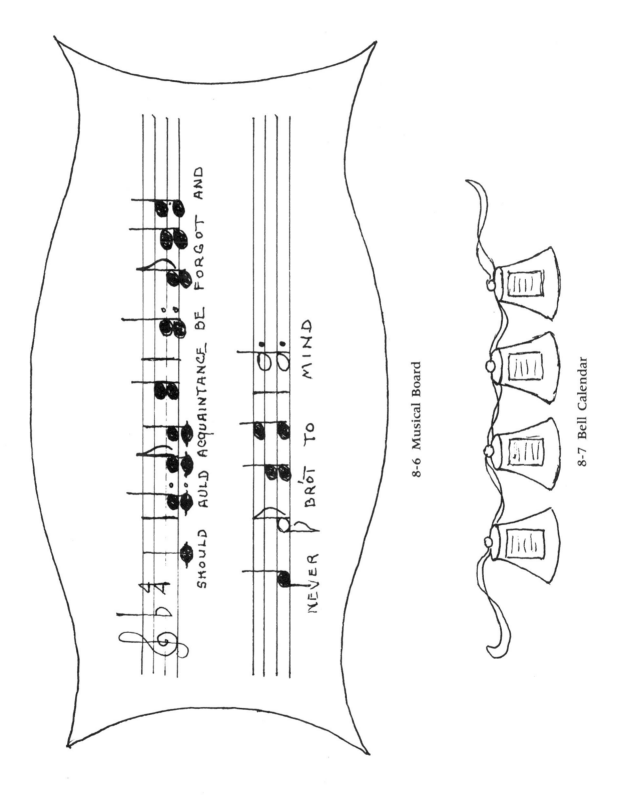

8-6 Musical Board

8-7 Bell Calendar

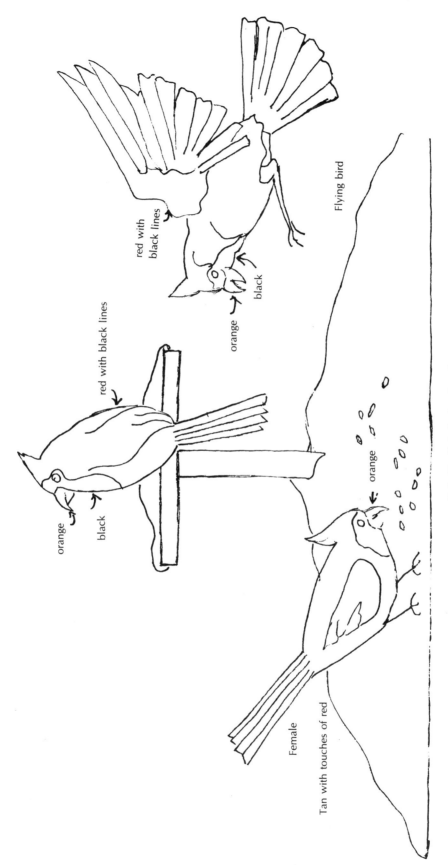

red with
black lines

red with black lines

black

orange

orange

black

Flying bird

orange

Female

Tan with touches of red

8-8 Redbirds in the Snow

133

Directions

1. Trace the bird forms on white construction paper; cut them out. Paint the redbirds with acrylic paint in red, orange and black.
2. If you prefer, the bird shapes may be cut from bright red art paper and the color added with orange and black acrylic paint.
3. Cut the post from grey construction paper with a bit of cut white paper on top for snow.
4. Cut the snow bank shape from gift wrap paper; spread on a bit of glue and sprinkle with artificial snow.
5. Real sunflower seed may be glued on the snow.
6. Position the birds on the background as shown in the drawings.

Calendar

The snowflake calendar suggested on page 131 is used with this bulletin board.

BULLETIN BOARD IDEAS FOR FEBRUARY

VALENTINES

Materials

Pierced hearts, birds or butterflies made in a previous craft session using patterns given in Part II;
Heavy corrugated cardboard or foam heart shape (from craft shop), 10 × 12 × 2 inches wide;
Utility knife to be used by director or volunteers;
Two inch wide strips of soft red fabric for the bulletin board-size heart—10 × 12 × 2 inches wide;
Scissors;
Wire cutter;
Soft white wire;
Red marker (color wire with marker);
Red and pink ½-inch ribbon—1½ yards red and 2 yards pink;
Dried babies' breath and small dried or artificial flowers;
Small piece of cotton batting (if using cardboard form).

To Do Ahead

Cut cardboard shape using pattern (Figure 8-9) or use a ready-made foam shape (Figure 8-10) for heart. If using cardboard, pad it with a small amount of batting cut to fit and glued to hold in place.

Directions

1. Wrap the strips of fabric on the diagonal, letting each strip overlap the previous strip a little. Most residents will be able to wrap.
2. After form is wrapped, add a bit of glue if necessary to hold in place.
3. Glue on the previously made pierced hearts or birds as shown in drawing.

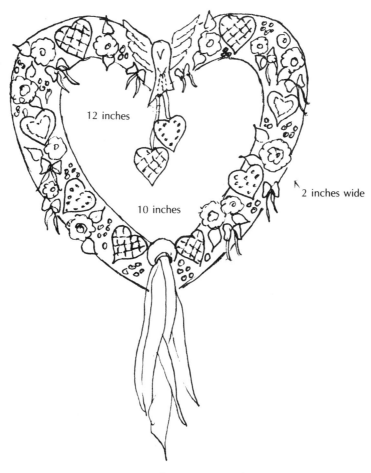

12 inches

10 inches

2 inches wide

8-9 Pierced Paper Wreath

4. Fill in the spaces with flowers, leaves, or dried materials by gluing or wiring with the soft white wire, colored with a red marker.
5. Fill in any remaining open spaces with tiny pink bows.
6. Long streamers of red ribbon can be knotted at the bottom of the heart if desired.

Calendar

Use white paper glued on a red doily heart or red and pink cut out hearts on white heart doilies.

Variation

A foam heart can be covered with fabric strips or ribbon wrapped on the diagonal and decorated with flowers and a red bow at the top. See Figure 8-10.

8-10 Foam Heart Covered with Fabric Strips,
Decorated with Artificial Flowers

VALENTINES

Materials

White poster board, 1 to 2 pieces, depending on size of project;
Red satin or felt, enough to cover the top heart piece;
Decorative braids, ribbons, and laces, long enough to fit across heart shape;
A strip of flower-patterned fabric long enough to reach across heart shape;
Black marker;
Glue;
Scissors;

To Do Ahead

From matching pieces of poster board (Figure 8-11), cut two heart shapes to fit your bulletin board.

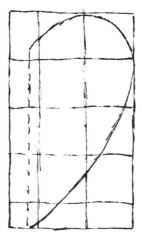

8-11 Heart Shape Pattern

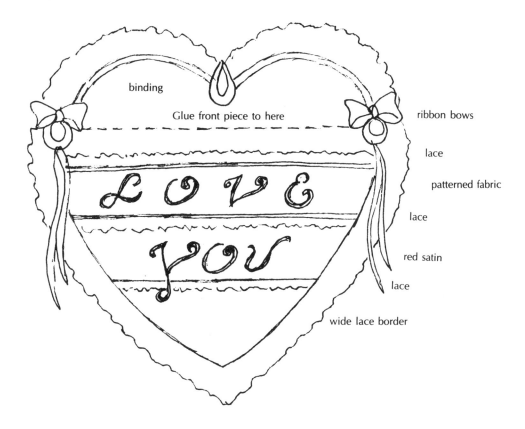

8-12 Pattern for Assembling

Directions

1. Cover the top heart piece with red satin or felt; cut the cover fabric ½ inch larger than heart shape; clip edges and fold over edge of heart, gluing down on back.
2. Decorate front with ribbon, braids, and patterned fabric as shown on drawing pattern (Figure 8-12).
3. Glue the two heart pieces together to the point shown on pattern. Leave top open for depositing valentines for residents.
4. Glue wide lace or gathered eyelet around entire edge of heart.
5. Tie bows at point shown.
6. Draw letters lightly on the two patterned pieces crossing the heart front and fill in with black marker.

Calendar

Use white paper glued on red heart doily or red or pink paper cut out hearts on white heart doilies (Figure 8-13).

8-13 Calendar

VALENTINES WITH TISSUE PAPER

Materials

Red poster board;
Pink and rose tissue paper;
Pencils with erasers;
White glue;
Scissors;
Two inch wide red ribbon—2½ yards for large bows;
One inch wide red ribbon—1 yard for streamers;
Narrow gathered lace—measure around edge of hearts and buy enough to glue to entire edge.

To Do Ahead

From poster board cut heart forms to fit your bulletin board.

Directions

1. Cut pink and rose tissue paper into about 1 inch squares.
2. Put glue on a small portion of the red heart base.
3. Place the eraser of a pencil in the middle of each square and fold the paper up around the pencil.
4. Press the tissue covered end of pencil into the glue; pull out pencil, leaving paper in place, keeping the squares very close together (Figure 8-14). Keep gluing a mixture of pink and rose squares until the hearts are covered. Most residents can help with this bulletin board.
5. Add large red bows and ribbon streamers; glue narrow gathered lace around edges.

Calendar

Directions are the same as previous bulletin boards for Valentines.

MARDI GRAS MASKS

Materials

Shiny black poster board for masks;
Crepe paper in contrasting colors—red, gold, silver, white;
Sequins, bits of gold or silver foil, feathers, artificial flowers, laces, and fake jewels to use for decoration on masks;
Glue;
Stapler;
Scissors.

fill in with tissue squares

lace or
eyelet borders

8-14 Double Hearts with Tissue Paper Filling

To Do Ahead

Using the full-sized pattern (Figure 8-15), cut 2 pieces of black poster board back to back (staple together before cutting, to hold) and cut out eye holes to match exactly in both pieces.

Directions

1. From across the bottom of the roll cut a strip of crepe paper 1½ inches wide; gently stretch one edge to form ruffling.
2. Apply a line of glue all around the back of one of the mask pieces and place the crepe frill or ruffling on it. Glue the other piece of mask over the ruffle to match the first piece.
3. Decorate the front of mask with sequins, or some of the other decorative materials listed above. Feathers, bows, jewels, flowers are all lovely (Figure 8-16).
4. Tie narrow ribbon in a bow to use at the top right corner, allowing streamers to hang down. See pattern.
5. A group of masks arranged on a bulletin board makes a very colorful collage.

Calendar

Use small cut paper masks for a calendar.

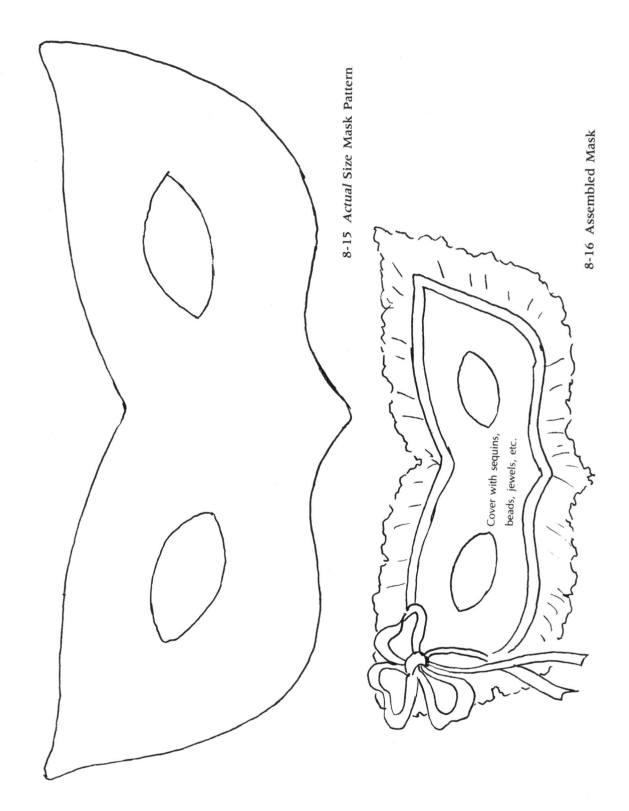

8-15 *Actual Size Mask Pattern*

8-16 *Assembled Mask*

Cover with sequins, beads, jewels, etc.

140

Spray gold or silver

Foam base covered with gold or silver paper

8-17 Table Setting Ideas

Variation

See patterns above (Figure 8-17) for ideas for table settings.

BULLETIN BOARD IDEAS FOR MARCH

KITES—ESPECIALLY APPEALING TO MEN

Materials

Poster board in any desired color or white for painting;
Brightly colored acrylic paint;
Brushes;
Glue (if making original kites);
Scissors;
Cords or string;
Fabric strips for tie-ons.

To Do Ahead

Trace and enlarge patterns (Figure 8-18) 4 or 5 times with pantograph. If anyone is interested in making an original kite, check the local library for ideas and patterns.

Directions

1. Cut kite shapes from poster board.
2. Paint designs on the kites with bright acrylic colors.

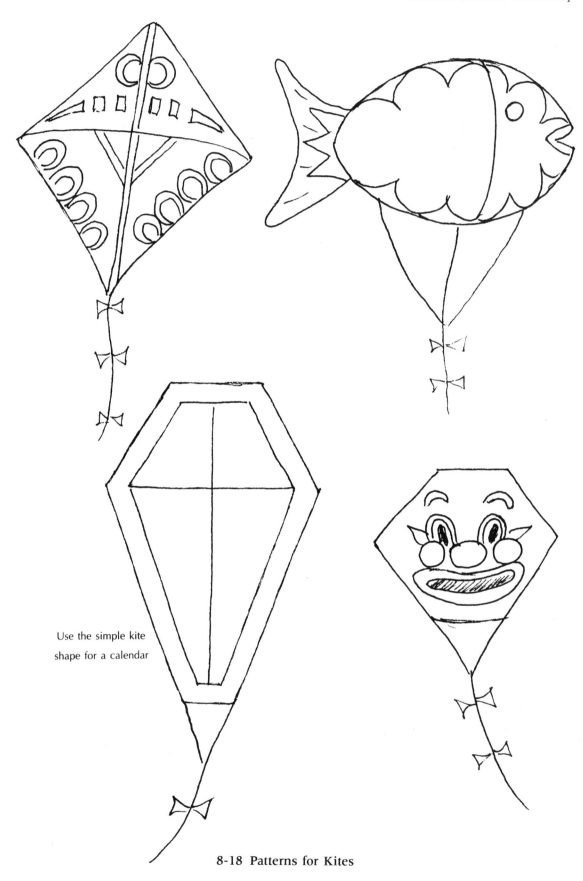

Use the simple kite
shape for a calendar

8-18 Patterns for Kites

3. Attach cords and tie-on strips by gluing.
4. Arrange on bulletin board.

Calendar

The kite shape shown in the drawing (Figure 8-18) makes a nice calendar. It should be enlarged about 1½ times.

SHAMROCK AND LEPRECHAUNS OR TREES IN WIND

Materials

White construction or art paper;
Acrylic paint—green, black, tan, or light brown for leprechaun;
Black and brown markers for leprechaun and trees;
Brushes;
Scissors;
Green construction paper for shamrocks;
Grey or brown poster board for trees;
Blue construction paper for bird shapes.

To Do Ahead

With pantograph, trace and enlarge leprechaun or tree shapes 4 or 5 times (or to suit your bulletin board space).

Directions

1. *Leprechaun:* Cut from white construction or art paper in a large size, being sure all inside lines are drawn in for a pattern (Figure 8-19).
2. Paint leprechaun face and hands and the mushroom shape a tan or light brown color, his suit green, and his hat and boots black; leave beard white.
3. Draw lines on face, hat, and suit with black marker and lines on mushroom with brown marker.
4. *Trees:* cut shapes from grey or brown poster board and add any lines with black or brown markers (Figure 8-21).
5. Cut bird shapes from blue construction or art paper and attach all shapes to bulletin board.

Calendar

Use drawing of shamrock (Figure 8-20) enlarged two times as a pattern for the calendar.

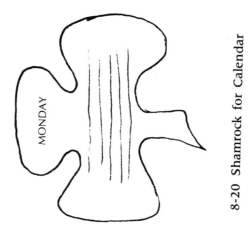

MONDAY

8-20 Shamrock for Calendar

8-19 Leprechaun

144

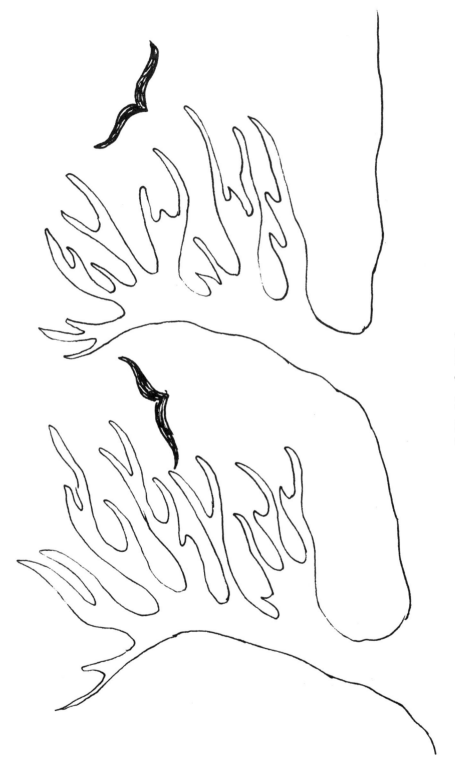

8-21 March Winds

BULLETIN BOARD IDEAS FOR MARCH, APRIL, AND MAY

HUMMINGBIRDS

Materials

Brightly colored art paper—blue, green, purple, red and rose—or white poster board to be
   painted with acrylic paint;
Bright acrylic paints in colors listed above (if using paint instead of paper);
Brushes;
Fine-line black marker; deep red marker;
Gold or colored glitter for iridescence;
Scissors;
Glue;
Pictures of hummingbirds as a guide for color placement.

To Do Ahead

Trace and enlarge patterns with pantograph to twice their size (or a size suitable for your bulletin
board).

Directions

1. Cut the bird shapes from brightly colored paper and the hibiscus from rose-colored paper. Or,
   cut the shapes from white paper or poster board and paint with bright acrylic colors, using
   hummingbird pictures as a guide for color placement (Figure 8-22).
2. Mark lines on the birds with a fineline black marker and the lines on the hibiscus with the
   deep red marker.
3. Add touches of gold or colored glitter for iridescence.
4. Cut leaves and stems for hibiscus from green paper; make lines with black marker.
5. Arrange in a pleasing design on the bulletin board.

Calendar

Use any simple flower shape for the calendar. Tulip shape or five-petal flower shape in Figure
8-23 should be enlarged twice.

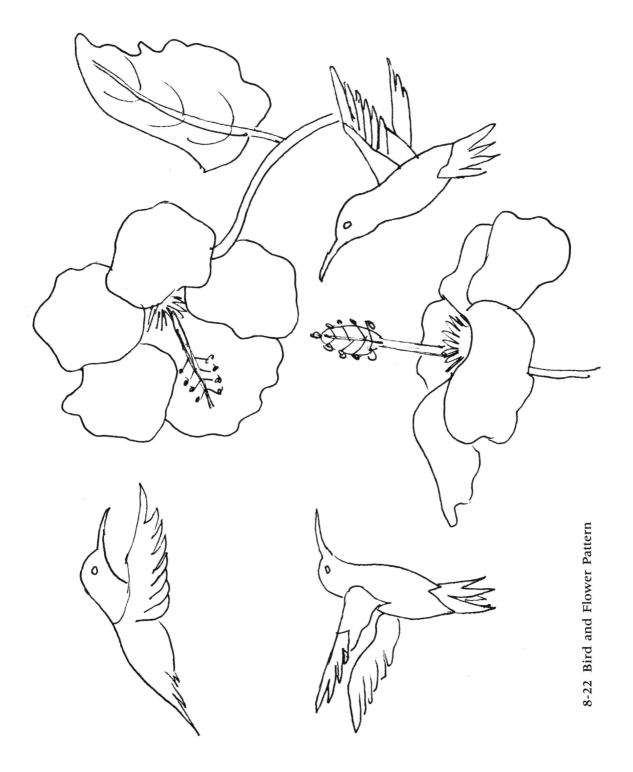

8-22 Bird and Flower Pattern

147

8-23 Simple Shapes for Calendar

WREN AND NEST

Materials

Construction or art paper—tan, rusty brown, dark brown, small amount of black; red clay color
for pot;
Scissors;
Glue;
Black marker;
Small piece of string.

To Do Ahead

Enlarge the wren and pot pattern (Figure 8-24) about 2 or 3 times, using the pantograph. Be sure
the size fits your bulletin board.

Directions

1. Cut the whole shape of the bird from tan or rusty brown paper; cut the smaller parts as
   indicated on the pattern from dark brown paper; glue on as shown on the drawing.
2. Use black marker to make lines and a black eye on the bird.
3. Cut black paper legs; glue on.
4. Cut a small piece of string to hang from the bird's beak.
5. Cut the pot from red clay-colored paper and glue bird to proper place on rim. Add a few dark
   lines to the pot.

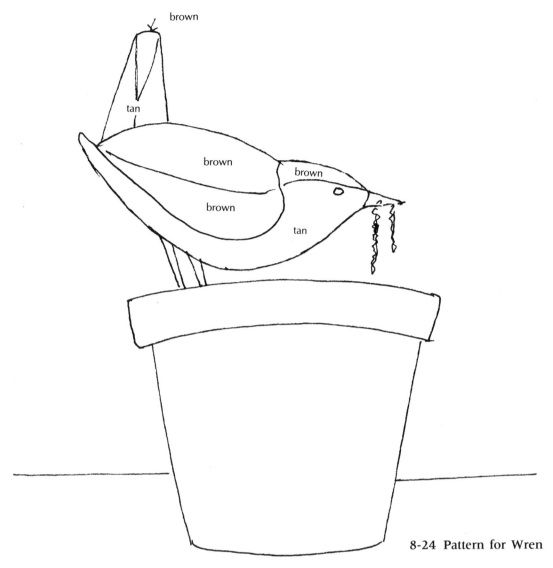

8-24 Pattern for Wren

Calendar

Tear irregular pieces of newspaper and glue a white rectangle of paper on it for printing the calendar (Figure 8-25). Wrens often use bits of paper in their nests.

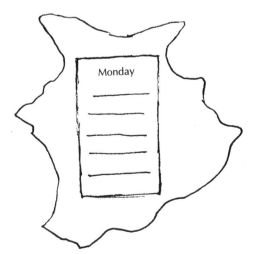

8-25 Calendar: Torn Newspaper with Printing on White Paper

EASTER HATS

Collect old hats from friends and relatives and have an Easter parade. Let the residents model the hats; take slides to show later. Give a prize for the most beautiful and the funniest.

Materials for Bulletin Board Hats—Women's

One 6-inch plastic foam ball (will make two hats);
Medium-weight cardboard for brims;
Fabric to cover brim and foam top;
Trims—laces, ribbons, artificial flowers;
Glue;
Sharp knife for cutting foam ball (director only);
Scissors.

To Do Ahead

Cut the foam ball in half. Cut a 14 × 18-inch oval shape for the brims (Figure 8-26).

Directions

1. Cover the half ball with soft fabric, clipped at the edges, turned under and glued down on bottom of ball half.
2. Cut a piece of fabric to fit brim shape plus ¼ inch all around; place over the oval shape, clip edges and glue down securely on back.
3. Place covered half ball in exact center of brim and glue down.
4. Decorate hat as desired with laces, braids, ribbons, flowers, feathers (Figure 8-26). Let long ribbon streamers hang down.

Materials—Men's Hats

Round, 6 inch diameter box;
Medium-weight cardboard for brim;
Paper for covering hat in any desired color;
Solid or striped ribbon—1½ yards;
Glue;
Scissors.

To Do Ahead

Cut circle 12 inches in diameter from cardboard.

Directions

1. Cover the round box (top and sides) with colored paper.
2. Cover circle for brim with the same color, gluing securely.
3. Glue box in center of brim, add a solid or striped ribbon band and bow.

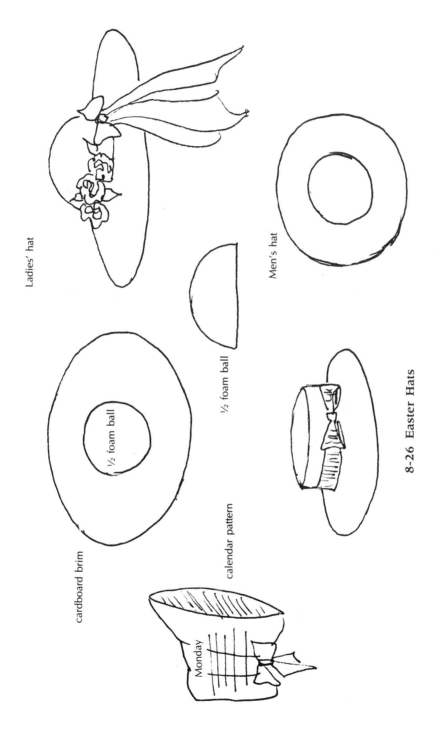

Ladies' hat

Men's hat

cardboard brim

½ foam ball

½ foam ball

calendar pattern

Monday

8-26 Easter Hats

151

Variation

The board may be decorated with a collection of several inexpensive floppy straw hats, and decorated as above.

Calendar

Use the bonnet pattern (p. 151, Figure 8-26), enlarged 2 or 3 times to fit your space.

APRIL SHOWERS

Materials

> Poster board in pastel colors (or all red for umbrellas);
> Grey construction paper (if using raindrops);
> Black marker;
> Pastel ribbons, 1½ yards for each umbrella;
> Small pastel artificial flowers;
> Glue or stapler;
> Scissors.

To Do Ahead

Trace and enlarge umbrella pattern, using pantograph. Enlarge four times or as required for your space.

Directions

1. If using raindrops, cut drop shapes from grey construction paper and draw faces on some with a black marker.
2. Cut the umbrella shapes from poster board. Pink, blue and yellow are good choices for colors. Cut handles separately and glue on back of umbrella.
3. Color the handles with black marker and draw lines on the umbrella top with marker.
4. Attach two ribbon streamers and a small bunch of flowers to the top of the umbrella shape with glue or stapler; tie a bow of the same ribbon to the handle of the umbrella (Figure 8-27).

Calendar

Use small folded umbrella shape or any simple flower shape for the calendar (Figure 8-28). These can be cut from construction paper in a color to coordinate with the umbrella colors.

8-27 April Showers

EASTER EGGS

Materials

Art paper in brilliant colors for the eggs;
Decorative materials such as braids, ribbons, sequins, dots or paper stars, etc. or acrylic paints
    may be used to paint the designs;
Brushes (if acrylic paint is used);
Glue;
Scissors;
Green gift wrap paper for the grass.

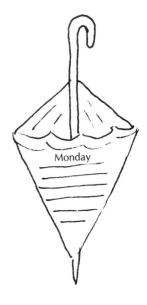

Monday

8-28 Calendar

8-29 Arrangement of Eggs for Bulletin Board

To Do Ahead

Trace and enlarge egg shape. Use pantograph or draw an enlarged oval shape at least 4 inches in length.

Directions

1. Trace the egg shapes onto brightly colored paper and let residents or others cut out; glue on the trims or paint the designs on the egg shapes with acrylic paint.
2. Arrange the eggs in an arrangement similar to the one shown in the drawing (Figure 8-29).
3. Cut jagged grass from a strip of green gift wrap paper; glue or staple across the bottom of the eggs.
4. A rabbit may be used beside the eggs if desired, but be sure it is an appropriate size for the egg arrangement.

Calendar

Use egg shapes in pastel colors for the calendar.

BUTTERFLIES

Materials

Art paper in bright colors;
Soft white wire;
Glue;
Colored waterproof markers, to use for making design patterns on butterfly wings;
Scissors.

To Do Ahead

Trace and enlarge the butterfly patterns to twice their size with the pantograph. The pattern cut on the fold is the shape which will be used with the wire centers (Figure 8-30).

Directions

1. Cut out the enlarged butterflies. One pattern is cut on the fold. Cut two of this butterfly so that the two sides can be glued together with wires between for shaping. Cut as many as you will need for your bulletin board space.
2. After the two matching shapes are cut, decorate the upper side of the wings with the colored markers to create the design pattern on the wing.
3. On the duplicate shape, glue a straight wire down the center of the body, extending a few inches beyond the end of body. Then glue cross wires as shown on the drawing (Figure 8-31) across the body. Glue on the decorated piece carefully; let dry; bend and shape the wings to look real. Group on bulletin board. Several side view butterflies look good mixed in with the wired ones.

8-31 Guide for Crosswires

Calendar

The profile shape can be enlarged one and a half times for a calendar. A simple flower shape is also very effective when used with the butterflies.

FLOWER CART

Materials

Colored construction or art paper—pink, red, yellow, white and green. Use brown, tan or rust colors for pots;
Colored markers for lines and flower centers—orange, gold, and black;
Glue;
Scissors;
Stapler.

To Do Ahead

Using the pantograph, trace and enlarge flowers and cart to desired size for your bulletin board.

Directions

1. Cut the pot shapes from brown, tan, or rust-colored paper.
2. Cut flowers from the colors indicated on the pattern (Figure 8-32); cut the leaves from green paper. Glue or staple together.

fold

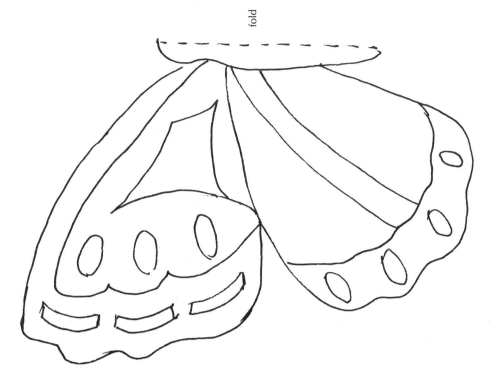

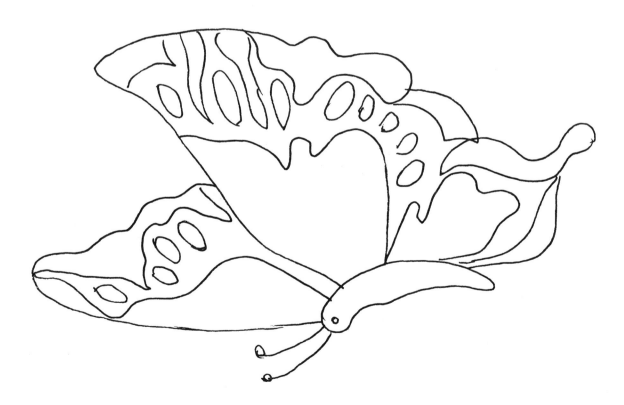

8-30 Butterfly

156

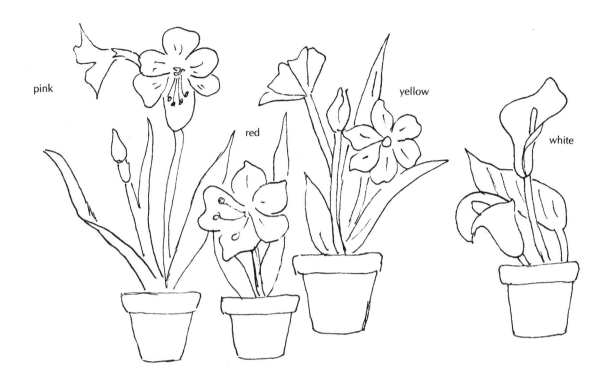

pink

red

yellow

white

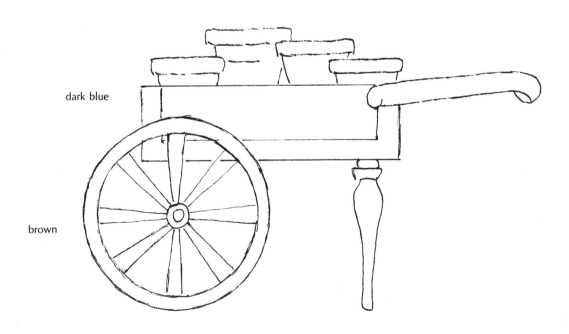

dark blue

brown

8-32 Flower Cart Patterns

3. Cut the cart from deep blue paper or poster board; cut the wheel from brown paper; glue together.
4. Mark lines on flowers with orange or gold markers; mark lines on the cart and wheel with black marker.
5. The flowers and pots will overlap each other when placed in the cart, so glue or staple them together when arranging them on the bulletin board.

Calendar

Use a flower shape (such as a lily) or a butterfly shape for the calendar. Butterflies are really nice with this bulletin board.

NOSEGAYS

Materials

White poster board;
Six 4-inch white paper doilies for each nosegay;
One 6-inch white paper doily for each nosegay;
A three-inch plastic foam ball (one ball will make two nosegays);
Tacky glue;
Scissors;
Stapler;
Knife for cutting plastic ball;
Short-stemmed artificial flowers—any desired colors;
Three yards of narrow ribbon for streamers for one nosegay.

To Do Ahead

Cut 10-inch circles from white poster board for each nosegay; slit from edge to center (Figure 8-33). Cut plastic balls in half with knife.

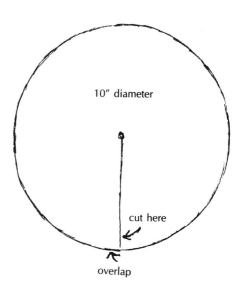

10″ diameter

cut here

overlap

8-33 Circle Pattern

Directions

1. Lap the edges of the cut circle about three inches on the edge and staple together to form an open cup shape.
2. Cover the shape with the four-inch doilies around the edge, overlapping slightly to form a lacy border. Let them extend a little over the edge of the circle. Glue down.
3. Then cover the center of the form with the six-inch doily; glue down.
4. With tacky glue, glue one half of a 3-inch plastic foam ball to the center of the shape; let it dry, curved side down (Figure 8-34).
5. Cut stems of artificial flowers short enough to stick in foam ball until shape is covered over six inches of center.
6. Tie three or four loops of narrow ribbons to match the flowers onto a piece of wire and stick this into bottom of foam ball so they hang down as long as desired (Figure 8-35).

Calendar

For the calendar use a flower or butterfly shape.

lapped circle

cut away

to fit into cup shape

8-34 Assembly   8-35 Finished Nosegay

BULLETIN BOARD IDEAS FOR JUNE

BASEBALL—FOR MEN

Materials

Heavy poster board or balsa wood for bats;
Brown marker for bats; other colors for marking team names on caps;
Colored paper for cap shapes (or use real baseball caps); use white paper for baseballs on calendar;
Black marker for lines on baseball;
Scissors.

To Do Ahead

Use the pantograph to trace and enlarge the bat pattern (enlarge cap patterns if not using real caps).

Directions

1. Cut bat shapes from heavy poster board or from thin balsa wood, if available (Figure 8-36).

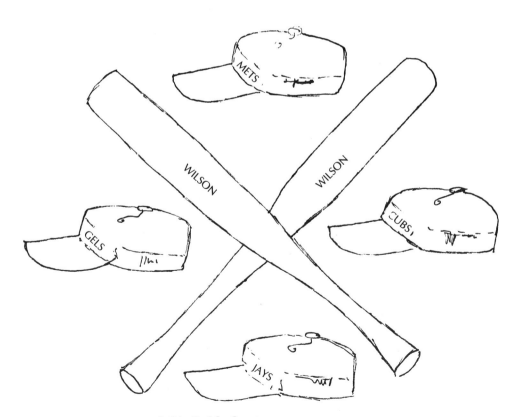

8-36 Guide for Arrangement

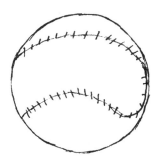

8-37 For Bulletin Board Activity Calendar

2. Mark a few lines on the bats and write a name with brown marker.
3. Use real caps or cut the shapes from colored paper and print names of teams on the caps with colored markers.
4. The men might be asked to name their favorite teams and decorate caps accordingly. If the residents watch an afternoon game on the television, you might serve peanuts, popcorn, and soda pop.

Calendar

For the calendar, cut the baseballs from white construction paper and draw seam lines with a black marker (Figure 8-37).

BOAT OR DOLPHIN AND WAVES

Materials

White and grey poster board;
Acrylic paints—red, blue and yellow (grey for dolphin);
Three shades of blue art or construction paper—light, medium, and very dark;
Black marker;
Glue;
Scissors;
Paint brushes.

To Do Ahead

Trace and enlarge patterns for boat and waves (Figure 8-38) or for dolphin and waves (Figure 8-39), using pantograph. Enlarge to a size suitable for your bulletin board.

Directions

1. Cut the boat shape from white poster board. With acrylic paints, paint colors indicated on pattern.
2. Draw lines on the white boat with black marker; shade the inside of the boat with black marker as shown.
3. If using the dolphin, cut the shape from grey poster board or cut from white poster board and paint with grey acrylic paint.

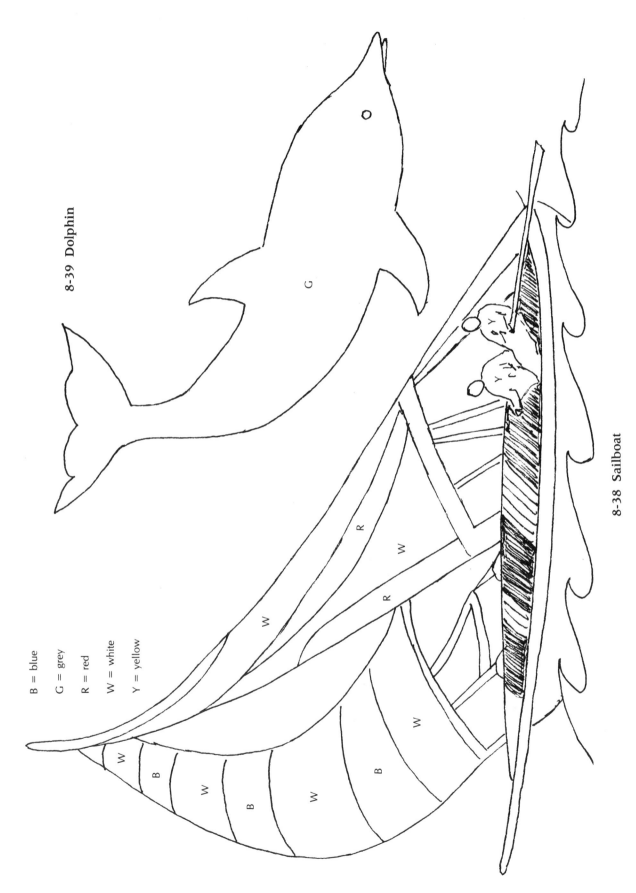

8-39 Dolphin

8-38 Sailboat

B = blue
G = grey
R = red
W = white
Y = yellow

162

top wave—light blue

second wave—medium blue

third wave—dark blue

8-40 Wave Pattern

163

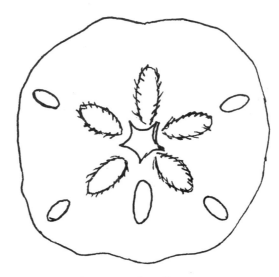

8-41 Sand Dollar

4. The wave pattern (Figure 8-40) at the base of the boat or dolphin is cut from the three shades of blue paper. Cut in three separate pieces and glue together.
5. This bulletin board is especially pleasing to men.

Calendar

Use the sand dollar (Figure 8-41) or one of the shells (Figure 8-42) for the calendar. Cut the sand dollar from light tan paper; cut shell from white or pale peach paper and mark lines with a colored marker.

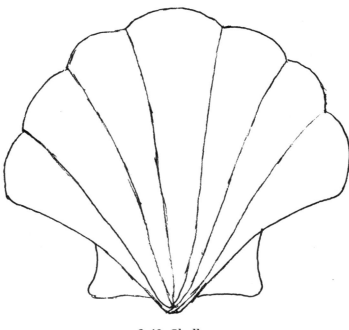

8-42 Shell

STATUE OF LIBERTY

Materials

White poster board or pale green heavy art paper;
Grey-green acrylic paint, if using white poster board; red acrylic paint for flag stripes;
Brushes;
Deep green marker;
Scissors.

To Do Ahead

Trace and enlarge the statue and flag (Figure 8-43) in one drawing if using poster board and acrylic paint. Enlarge and cut separately if using green art paper, cutting flag from white poster board. Enlarge 6 to 8 times for most bulletin board space.

8-43 Statue of Liberty

Directions

1. Cut the pattern from the poster board, paint the statue with grey-green acrylic paint *before* drawing in all the lines with a permanent dark green marker. Paint flag stripes red.
2. Or cut the pattern from pale green art paper; draw in dark green lines and place against the flag (cut from white poster board with stripes painted on in red acrylic paint).
3. Mount on bulletin board as shown in drawing.

Calendar

The Liberty bell pattern (Figure 8-44) makes a wonderful calendar for use with the Statue of Liberty. Stars may also be used (Figure 8-45).

8-44 Bell Pattern for Activity Calendar   8-45 Star Pattern for Activity Calendar

INDEPENDENCE HALL AND PREAMBLE TO THE CONSTITUTION

Materials

White poster board;
Acrylic paint—pink and deep rose for building; black for roof;
Black marker;
Thin paper for scroll;
Scissors;
Stapler.

To Do Ahead

With pantograph trace and enlarge the pattern on white poster board.

Directions

1. Cut the enlarged pattern from white poster board. Paint the building pale pink on the side sections and the center section deep rose. The roof and window and door openings are black (Figure 8-46).
2. For the scroll, cut a 15 × 18-inch piece of thin white paper; roll at the ends as shown in the drawing (Figure 8-47).

8-46 Independence Hall

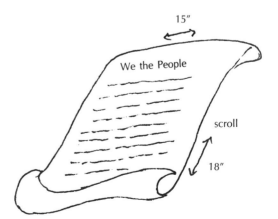

8-47 Preamble to the Constitution

3. Copy the preamble (the script for heading is shown actual size) on the paper, *continuing with small script until entire preamble is on scroll* (Figure 8–48).
4. Place the scroll at the base of the building.

Calendar

Use Liberty Bell or stars for calendar (Figures 8-44, 8-45).

8-48 Actual Size of Script for Scroll Heading

BULLETIN BOARD IDEAS FOR JUNE, JULY OR AUGUST

WATERMELONS

Materials

White poster board or deep rose red art paper for watermelons;
Rose red acrylic paint for melons and green acrylic paint for the outside of melon, black for seeds
  (or use real seeds);
Black marker can also be used for seeds;
Scissors;
Glue (if using real seeds).

To Do Ahead

Trace and enlarge pattern of double melons (Figure 8-49) with pantograph, enlarging 4 times (or
desired size for your bulletin board).

Directions

1. Cut the enlarged pattern from the rose red art paper or from the white poster board.
2. If using poster board, paint the center section of the melon with rose red paint, leave a white
   stripe and then add a green stripe along the edge of melon.
3. Place the two melons at right angles on the bulletin board.

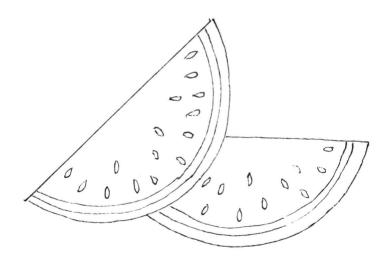

8-49 Double Melons

Calendar

For the calendar, use the melon pattern that is cut on the fold (Figure 8-50). Cut these from rose pink construction paper; paint a green border with a green marker; and write on them with black. Place them on the bulletin board at an angle as shown (Figure 8-51) for a very effective calendar and board.

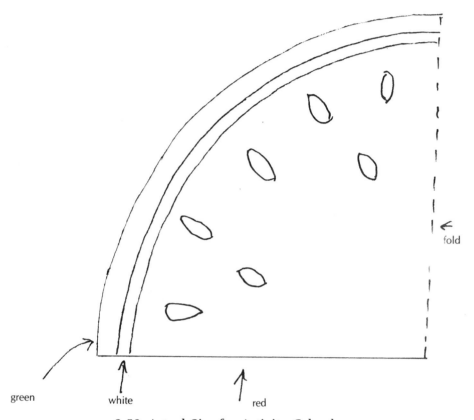

fold

green   white   red

8-50 Actual Size for Activity Calendar

8-51 Arrangement for Bulletin Board Activity Calendar

ICE-CREAM CONES—SUMMER TIME FUN (NATIONAL ICE CREAM WEEK: JULY 10–16)

Materials

Colored construction paper—brown for chocolate; pink for strawberry; pale yellow for vanilla; red for cherry; tan for the ice-cream cones;
Brown marker for marking on cones; matching markers for ice cream;
Scissors;
Glue.

To Do Ahead

Enlarge the two pointed cone patterns (Figure 8-52) to twice their size with the pantograph, separating the ice cream cones from the cone bottoms so you have the two patterns.

8-52 Ice Cream Cones

Directions

1. Cut the ice cream tops from the various colored papers; mark lines on pink paper with red marker, brown paper with deep brown marker and on pale yellow paper with yellow marker.
2. Cut the cone shape from tan paper; mark on the cone with the brown marker.
3. Glue the ice cream in place on the cones and arrange on the bulletin board, using about five cones in a pleasing arrangement.
4. It would be fun to serve ice cream sometime during National Ice Cream Week (July 10–16).

Calendar

For the calendar use the cup-shaped cone, shown actual size for using on the activity calendar (Figure 8-53). Cut the tan paper and draw lines with brown marker; print calendar with brown marker.

8-53 Actual Size for Activity Calendar

OLD-FASHIONED FANS: MEMORY BOARD

Materials

Construction paper in any colors desired for fans. Paper will need to be at least 12 × 18 inches;
Colored markers in colors of fans, only deeper;
Acrylic paints;
Brushes;
Scissors;
Small craft sticks;
Glue;
Ribbon—½ inch wide, about ¾ yard for each fan.

To Do Ahead

Trace and enlarge fan pattern on pantograph to about twice the size. This is the semicircular part of the fan (Figure 8-54).

Directions

1. Draw around the enlarged pattern on the colored construction paper and cut out the semi-circular forms. Draw fold lines on the fan with the markers and paint a floral design on the fan with acrylic paint.
2. Small craft sticks can be glued to the base of the fan shape, overlapping them at the lower point as shown in drawing. Glue securely together at the point.
3. Add the bow at the bottom of fan. Real fans can be used if available.
4. Make three fans for the board and arrange as shown (Figure 8-55).
5. Most of the residents used fans like these at one time in their lives. They might be asked to describe the fans they used. Most will mention the fans presented by local funeral homes to area churches. These fans could be found in every pew.

Calendar

Use the old palm fan pattern (Figure 8-56) shown actual size for the calendar. Cut from tan construction paper; use brown markers to make lines. Glue a small wooden spoon handle to the back of fan (Figure 8-57).

BULLETIN BOARD IDEAS FOR AUGUST OR SEPTEMBER

CIRCUS THEME

National Clown Week is August 1–7. Many of these patterns may also be used for a circus theme party as suggested in the party section of this book, Part VII.

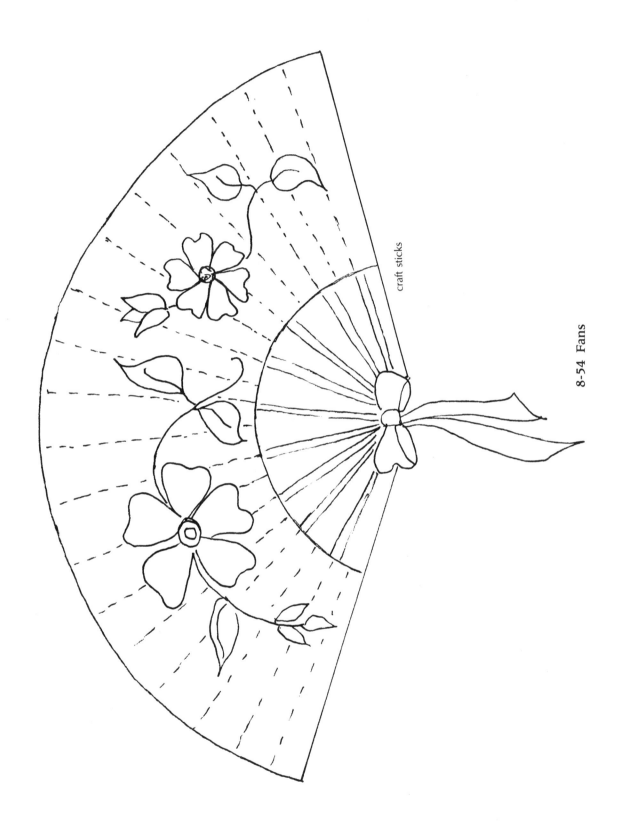

craft sticks

8-54 Fans

8-55 Arrangement on Bulletin Board

8-57 Wooden Spoon for Handle

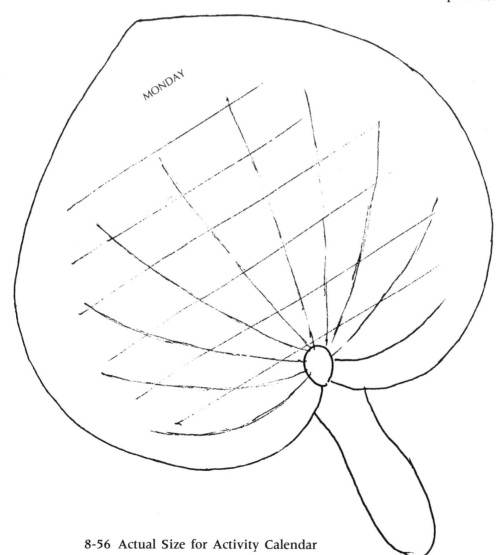

MONDAY

8-56 Actual Size for Activity Calendar

Materials

White poster board;
Acrylic paint in bright colors;
Brushes;
Glue;
Decorative materials: fancy papers, buttons, pompoms, artificial flowers;
Colored markers;
Scissors.

To Do Ahead

Use the pantograph to trace and enlarge the desired patterns to a size to fit your bulletin board (probably 2 or 3 times).

Directions

1. Cut clowns or elephants from poster board after enlarging.
2. Paint clowns with bright colors; glue on the decorative materials (buttons, fancy paper, pompoms, flowers); add lines with colored markers (Figure 8-58).
3. Cut umbrella from poster board; add flower or pompom to top; place in clown's hand.
4. Cut elephant from poster board; paint grey. For the elephant on the ball (Figure 8-59), paint the ball with bright colors. For the decorated elephant (Figure 8-60), add braids, tassels, gold braid, etc.
5. Cut the circus wagon (enlarged twice) (Figure 8-61) from poster board.
6. Decorate the wagon with felt, rickrack, ribbons, sequins, and buttons as shown in drawing. Glue all of these materials on wagon; glue the wheels on in the proper place.
7. Cut bear from brown paper (Figure 8-62), use black marker for lines and tan pads on feet and nose.
8. Cut the lion's ruff and tail tip from orange paper, tan face and body, lines with black marker (Figure 8-63).
9. The animals should be placed in the cage of the wagon before adding the ribbon cage bars.

Calendar

Various colored balloons make a fine calendar to go with the circus theme. Enlarge calendar balloon (Figure 8-64) three times.

balloons

8-58 Clowns   8-59 Elephant on Ball

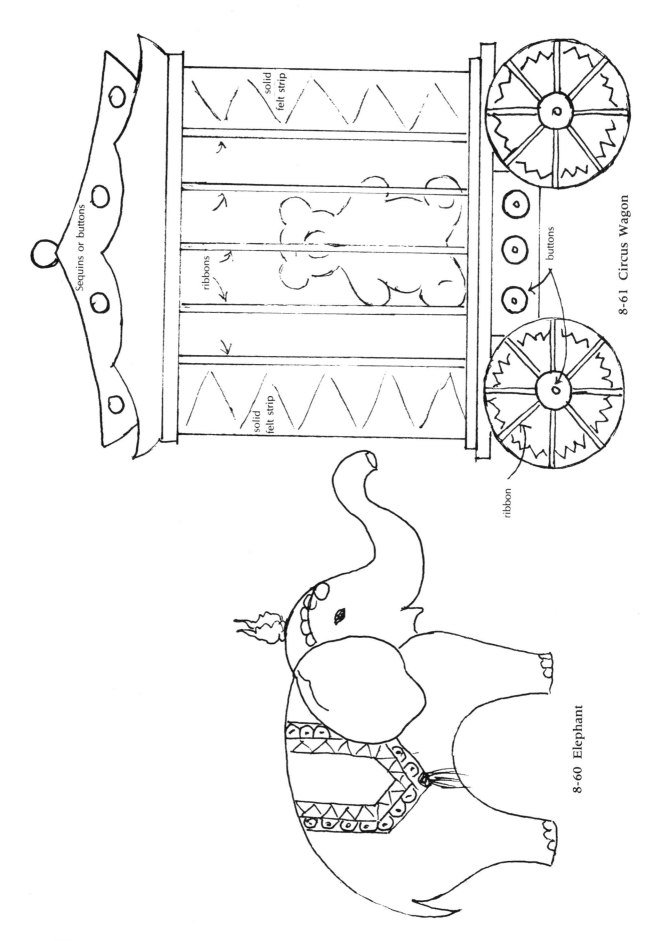

Sequins or buttons

solid
felt strip

ribbons

solid
felt strip

buttons

ribbon

8-61 Circus Wagon

8-60 Elephant

8-64 Calendar Balloon

8-63 Lion

8-62 Bear

BULLETIN BOARD IDEAS FOR SEPTEMBER OR OCTOBER

COUNTY FAIR

Materials

Patchwork squares made by the residents (as suggested in Part V);
Prize ribbons; blue, red and white;
Poster board for carousel horse;
Acrylic paints in bright colors;
Brushes;
Colored markers;
Button, gold braids, or other decorative materials to use on horse;
Glue;
Scissors.

To Do Ahead

Have residents make fabric patchwork squares (Figure 8-65). Use pantograph to trace and enlarge the horse 3 or 4 times (to a size to fit your bulletin board) (Figure 8-66).

Directions

1. Mount the patchwork squares on the bulletin board and attach a ribbon (Figure 8-67) near each one. Make the first prize ribbon blue; the second prize red; and the third white. See design guide for assembling the squares.
2. The horse can be mounted on the other side of the same board or used alone on the board with a county fair sign attached.
3. After horse is cut from poster board, paint with bright acrylic paint, or leave horse white with brightly painted trappings, adding decorative materials, buttons, gold braid.
4. Draw all lines on the horse with colored markers.

Calendar

For a patchwork squares bulletin board, use squares of white paper mounted on fabric squares at an angle. For the carousel horse, use a chain of little girls as shown in Part II; print the calendar on them.

This is a good memory-providing bulletin board. Ask questions about county fairs. "What do you remember about the county fair?" "Why did you like to go and what did you like best?" "Did you submit something to be judged? Food? Livestock? Crafts? Other?"

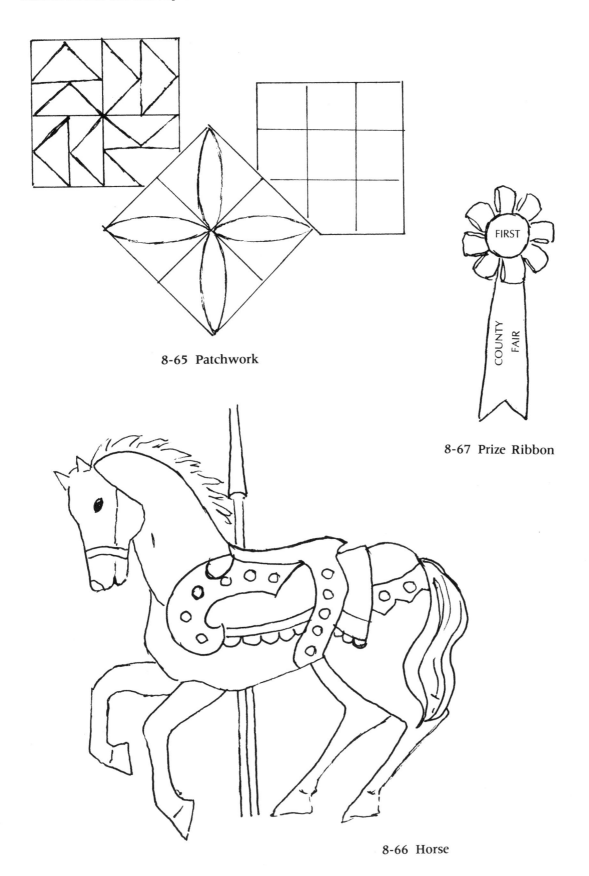

8-65 Patchwork

8-67 Prize Ribbon

8-66 Horse

BEGINNING OF SCHOOL

Materials

White poster board for building and tree;
Acrylic paints; red for building; grey or dark brown for doors and bell; green for tree and brown
   for trunk;
Brushes;
Glue;
Scissors;
Green gift wrap paper or green construction paper for grass.

To Do Ahead

Using pantograph trace and enlarge tree and schoolhouse about 4 times. Enlarge other shapes to
suit bulletin board.

Directions

1. Cut the enlarged schoolhouse and tree patterns from the white poster board (Figure 8-68).
2. Paint the schoolhouse red, and doors and bell (Figure 8-69) grey or brown, with acrylic
   paint.
3. Paint the tree top green or cover with a patterned green paper glued on. Paint the trunk grey or
   brown to match doors and bell.
4. Mount on bulletin board as shown in drawing.

Calendar

For the calendar, cut red apples (Figure 8-70) from art paper, add a brown stem and green leaf.

Variation

The bulletin board can be memory provoking by arranging red tablets with pencils attached by a
cord or grey slate boards with chalk and erasers attached with cords and with bells crossed over top
of board. This was the way it was when most of the residents went to school.

SCARECROW—APPEALS TO MEN

Materials

White poster board;
Acrylic paint; yellow for hat; two shades of blue for coat and pants;
Brushes;
Black marker;

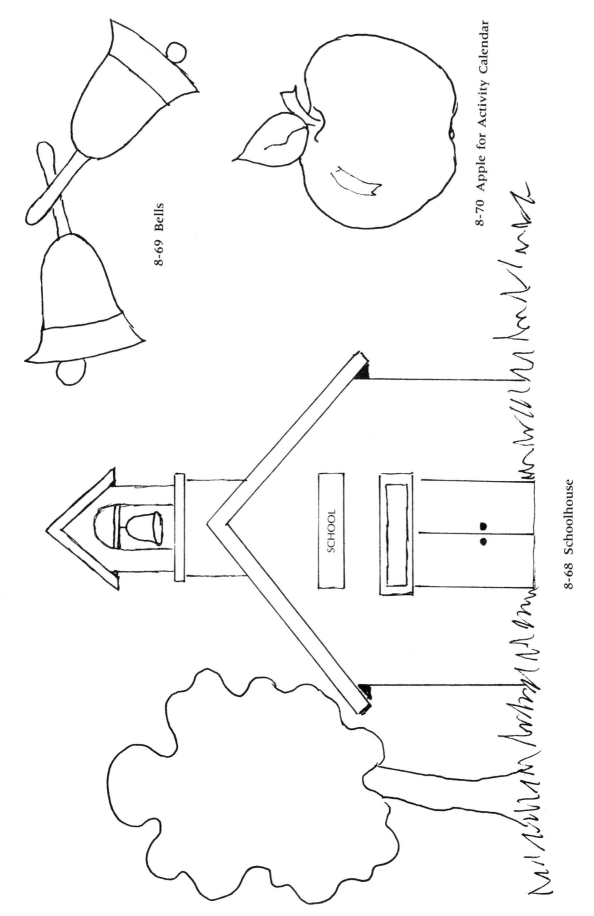

8-69 Bells

8-70 Apple for Activity Calendar

8-68 Schoolhouse

SCHOOL

183

Fabric patches for clothing;
Buttons for coat;
Glue;
Straw (if available);
Scissors;
Brown wrapping paper for grass and pole;
Orange paper for pumpkins.

To Do Ahead

Use pantograph to trace and enlarge drawing of scarecrow and pumpkins about twice (or a size suitable for your bulletin board).

Directions

1. Cut the enlarged drawing of the scarecrow (Figure 8-71) from white poster board. Cut the pumpkins (Figure 8-71) from orange poster board or orange paper.
2. Using the acrylic paint, paint the hat yellow, the pants dark blue, and the coat light blue. Glue on fabric patches and buttons.
3. Use real straw for hands and feet if available, or cut from tan paper and glue under the edge of coat sleeve and leg cuff.
4. Cut grass and pole from brown wrapping paper, and pumpkins from orange paper. Scatter pumpkins in grass.
5. Make lines on scarecrow face with black marker and mount all in place on bulletin board.

Calendar

Orange paper pumpkins make a lovely activity calendar to use with this bulletin board

HALLOWEEN

Materials

White or grey poster board;
Acrylic paint; grey and black;
White construction paper for ghosts, brown for tree and grass;
Glue;
Scissors;
Black marker;
Paint brushes.

To Do Ahead

Use pantograph to trace and enlarge the house and tree (Figure 8-72) two or three times, depending on the size of your bulletin board. Trace ghost on white construction paper to use in door.

8-71 Scarecrow and Pumpkins

8-72 Haunted House

Directions

1. Cut the house from gray poster board if available, or cut from white poster board and paint light grey with acrylic paint.
2. Paint the roof a deeper grey and the openings in the house, the doors, and parts of the windows black.
3. Make all the shadings and lines with a black marker.
4. Cut the tree and grass from brown construction paper. Cut the ghost in the door from white construction paper and glue on the house.
5. Arrange figures on the bulletin board as shown on the drawing.

Calendar

Using the ghost patterns (Figure 8-73), make enough ghosts for the calendar. Let the ghosts trail from the open door to the ghosts on the calendar.

Variation

Use the witch (Figure 8-73), enlarged 3 times, cut from the same white poster board. Paint hat black, dress grey, hair brown, shoes black. Cut a large round orange moon to go behind the witch's head; cut a broom from brown and tan construction paper. Glue the broom behind the witch and the moon behind her head and mount on bulletin board. Enlarge bat pattern 3 or 4 times and use as a calendar.

8-73A Ghosts for Activity Calendar

8-73B Witch and Bat

BULLETIN BOARD IDEAS FOR OCTOBER OR NOVEMBER

FOOTBALL THEME—APPEALS TO MEN

Materials

College and university pennants—a variety from colleges and universities in your area. Some
   may be borrowed from the community or small ones can often be found in local variety stores;
Or felt in various school colors, if you care to make your own pennants;
Scissors;
Glue (if making pennants).

To Do Ahead

Recruit people in the community to locate the pennants needed, probably three for each bulletin
board.

Directions

1. Mount the pennants in a pleasing design on the board. See Figure 8-74.

Calendar

Enlarge the football (Figure 8-75) drawing twice for the calendar; cut from light brown construction paper; draw black lines and white bands across ends.

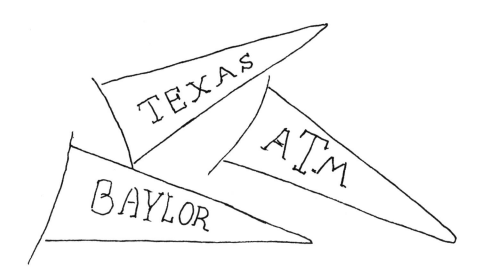

8-74 School Pennants—Guide to Arrangement

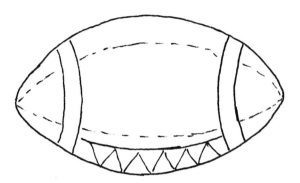

8-75 Football for Activity Calendar

This is a memory-provoking bulletin board. Ask questions: "Do you remember what football games were like when you were young? What did the playing field look like? What was different about the uniform worn by the players? Did any of your children play football? Did you play football" (if a man)? "Do you like today's games better or less than the old way?"

THANKSGIVING

Materials

White poster board for the figures;
Acrylic paint: black and grey;
Brushes;
Buttons in correct size for the man's coat—grey;
Black marker;
Scissors.

To Do Ahead

Use pantograph to trace and enlarge the figures at least three times (or to a size to fit your bulletin board.

Directions

1. Cut the figures from the white poster board (Figure 8-76).
2. With acrylic paint, paint the woman's clothing: black bodice and sleeves, leave collar, cap, cuffs and apron white. Paint shoes black and skirt grey.
3. For the man, paint suit and hat black, belt grey, buckle outlined with black marker. Glue on grey buttons. Leave collar and cuffs white; paint stockings grey and shoes black.
4. Draw all lines on both figures with black marker.
5. Mount on bulletin board.

Colors

W = white

B = black

G = grey

F = flesh

8-76 Thanksgiving Figures

Calendar

The turkey pattern (Figure 8-77) shown actual size makes a fine activity calendar to use with the pilgrims. Pumpkins can also be used very effectively.

8-77 Turkey Activity Calendar (Actual Size)

BULLETIN BOARD IDEAS FOR DECEMBER

SANTA

Materials

White poster board and gift wrap paper in various colors;
Acrylic paint: black, red, brown;
Brushes;
Red pompom;
Scissors;
Fake fur or cotton (if desired);
Glue.

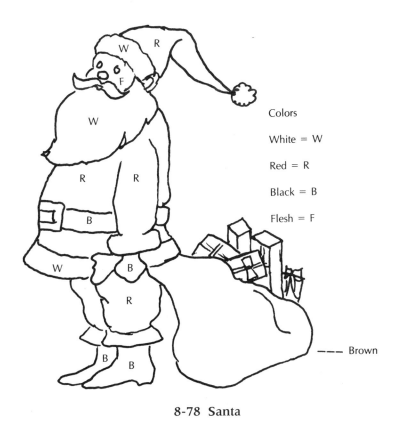

Colors

White = W

Red = R

Black = B

Flesh = F

——— Brown

8-78 Santa

To Do Ahead

Use pantograph to trace and enlarge the figure (Figure 8-78) three or four times (or to a size to fit your bulletin board).

Directions

1. Cut the figure from white poster board.
2. Paint parts as shown with acrylic paint.
3. Glue on fake white fur or cotton for beard and for fur on clothes (if desired). Otherwise, leave white poster board blank.
4. Cut bag shape; paint brown; add gift boxes cut from gift wrap paper. Glue ribbon on the outside.
5. Glue red pompom on tip of cap.
6. Mount on bulletin board.

Calendar

The stocking pattern (Figure 8-79) enlarged twice makes a good calendar to go with the Santa board. It should be cut from either red construction paper with black printing or white paper with red printing.

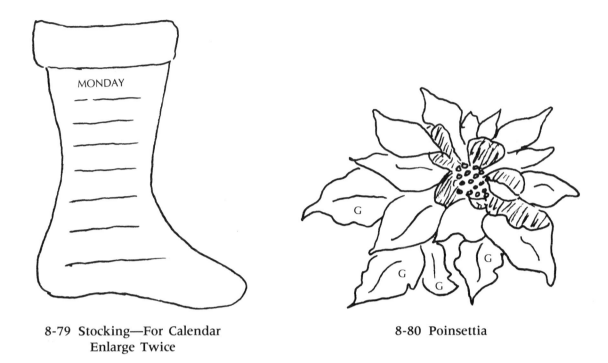

8-79 Stocking—For Calendar   8-80 Poinsettia
Enlarge Twice

POINSETTIA

Materials

Two shades of red felt, art paper, or acrylic paint for the flowers;
Green felt, art paper, or acrylic paint for leaves;
Yellow felt centers or ready-made floral centers;
Paint brushes (if using acrylics);
Scissors;
Glue.

To Do Ahead

Use pantograph to trace and enlarge the poinsettia pattern (Figure 8-80) three times (or to a size to fit your bulletin board).

Directions

1. Cut the entire leaf shape from the lighter shade of red material (or from white poster board, if you are painting). Cut the small section at the center, shown shaded in drawing, from the darker shade of red and glue over the first petal (or paint dark red, if painting).
2. Make three flowers for the bulletin board. Glue the yellow centers on in the proper place.
3. Cut the green leaves from the chosen material and glue into place at the base of the flower.
4. Mount on bulletin board.

Calendar

Cut Christmas tree chains as shown in Part II or simply cut Christmas tree patterns and print on them with white ink or red markers.

ANGELS

Materials for First Angel

White poster board;
Gold foil or gold spray paint;
Scissors;
Black marker.

Materials for Second Angel

White poster board;
Small amount of burlap or gold net;
Gold spray paint;
Black or brown felt for hair;
Red acrylic paint for letters;
Brushes;
Scissors;
Glue.

Materials for Third Angel

White poster board;
Bright colors of acrylic paint: deep greens, blues, reds, purple;
Brushes;
Gold foil or spray paint for horn; (wings and outer halo are gold);
Decorative trim;
Colored markers for all lines;
Sequins, glitter and fake jewels;
Scissors.

To Do Ahead

Trace any of the angel patterns and enlarge on the pantograph four to five times (or as needed to fit your bulletin board).

Directions for First Angel (Figure 8-81)

1. Cut shape from cardboard; cover with gold foil or spray paint with gold spray.
2. Draw the lines with black marker and mount on the bulletin board.

8-81 First Angel   8-82 Second Angel

Directions for Second Angel (Figure 8-82)

1. Cut the hair, horn, wings and letters from poster board.
2. Spray paint the wings gold if using gold net to cover. *Or* cover the wings with burlap, trimming the edges carefully.
3. Cut black or brown felt to fit the hair pattern and glue on the base pattern of poster board.
4. Spray paint the horn gold.
5. Paint the letters with red acrylic paint, or cut letters from bright red art paper.
6. Mount on bulletin board as shown in drawing.

Directions for Third Angel (Figure 8-83)

1. Cut the angel shape from the poster board.
2. Paint the designs on the angel with bright acrylic colors. Paint the wings, outer halo, and horn with gold paint.

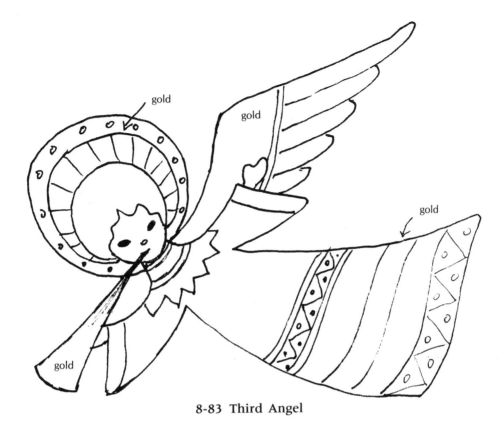

8-83 Third Angel

3. Draw all lines with markers in contrasting colors.
4. Glue on sequins, fake jewels, and glitter wherever you think they are needed. This is a very richly designed angel.
5. Mount on bulletin board.

LITTLE CHURCH

Materials

White poster board;
Acrylic paint: grey-blue or brown;
Brushes;
Black marker;
Green construction paper or art paper; red paper for holly berries;
Red ribbon, ¾ yard of ½ inch wide for bow on wreath;
Decorations for trees (whatever you desire or have available);
Scissors;
Glue.

To Do Ahead

Enlarge pattern (Figure 8-84) about three times, using the pantograph. Enlarge to appropriate size for your bulletin board.

8-84 Little Church

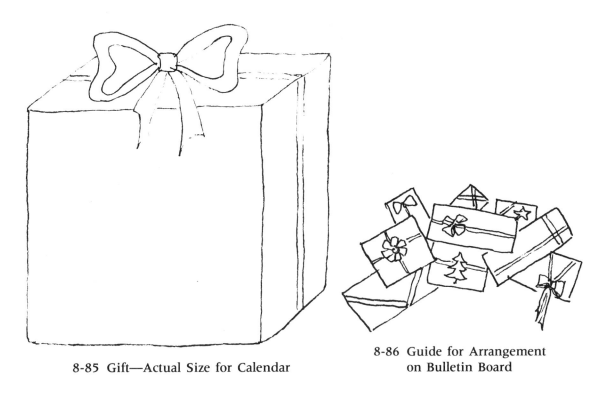

8-85 Gift—Actual Size for Calendar

8-86 Guide for Arrangement
on Bulletin Board

Directions

1. Cut the church from the poster board.
2. Paint the doors, windows, and upper louvers grey-blue or brown. Leave the church white.
3. Draw all lines with black marker.
4. Cut trees and wreaths from green paper; glue holly leaves to the wreath in a lighter shade of green, and add a few red berries.
5. Decorate the trees by glueing on small gold cord or small balls of colored paper (whatever you have available).
6. Mount on bulletin board.

Calendar

See star pattern (Figure 8-45, July bulletin boards) or bell pattern (Figure 8-7, January bulletin boards). You can also use small Christmas trees. The package pattern shown above (Figure 8-85) will be good for several of the December bulletin boards, including the Advent calendars suggested below. Cut from colored paper and tie with real ribbon.

Variations

Ten or twelve differently-shaped small boxes can be wrapped in Christmas paper or paper made by the residents, tied with pretty ribbons or cords, and arranged on the bulletin board (Figure 8-86).

Advent calendars can also be used as December bulletin boards. See Part VII for two ideas for Advent calendars.

The little houses along the street shown in this section, Part VIII, can be decorated for Christmas with trees, wreaths, etc., to make a Christmas bulletin board.

BULLETIN BOARD IDEAS FOR ANY MONTH

DEEP SEA DESIGNS

Materials

White poster board, or art paper in blue, green, purple, rose, yellow, and orange.
Or acrylic paint in blue, green, purple, rose, yellow, and orange.
Brushes;
Scissors;
Colored markers in deep shades of above colors, or black.

To Do Ahead

On the pantograph enlarge designs two or three times (or to a size right for your bulletin board).

Directions

1. Cut the shapes from white poster board or from colored art paper. If cutting from art paper, follow the basic colors indicated in the drawings.
2. If cutting shapes from white poster board, paint the designs with acrylic paint, following the basic colors shown in the drawings.
3. If using colored art paper, make the markings with colored markers.
4. The seaweed is in shades of green, the tropical fish in shades of yellow and orange, the angel fish is yellow with blue stripes, and the starfish is lavender with blue markings (Figure 8-87).
5. Mount the undersea shapes on the bulletin board.

Calendar

The calendar can be the shell (Figure 8-42) or sand dollar (Figure 8-41) shown in the June bulletin board.

MUSICAL INSTRUMENTS

Materials

White poster board;
Acrylic paint in various shades of brown;
Black marker;
Old sheet music (if available);
Gold spray paint;
Small pushpins;
Strings or Wires (if desired);
Scissors.

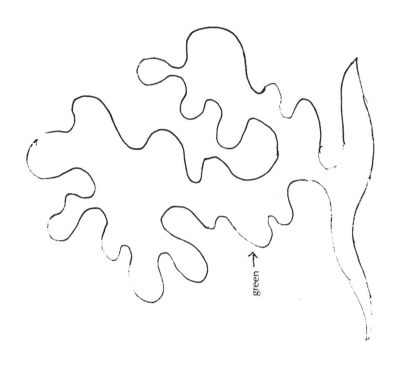

green

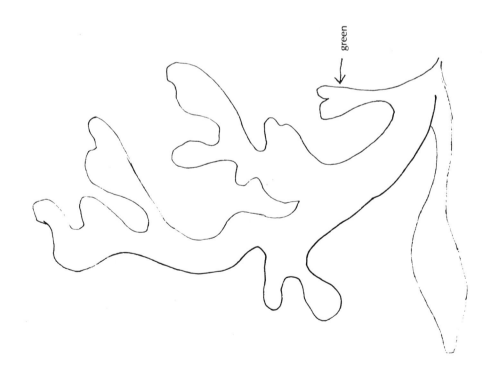

green

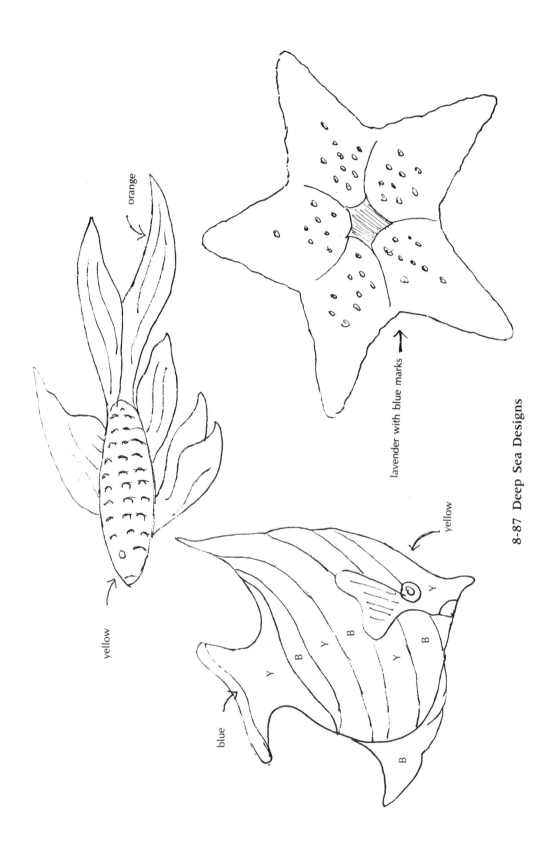

orange

yellow

blue

lavender with blue marks

yellow

8-87 Deep Sea Designs

To Do Ahead

On the pantograph enlarge patterns (Figure 8-88) three times (or to a size needed for your bulletin board).

8-88 Musical Instruments

8-89 Sheet Music   8-90 Calendar—White Paper Glued on Old Music

Directions

1. Cut the enlarged shapes from white poster board.
2. Spray paint any wind instruments with gold spray paint and paint the string instruments with various shades of brown acrylic paint.
3. If you want the string instruments to look more real, use six pushpins at the bottom and top of the instrument as shown on the drawing and attach tiny wires or strings to them.
4. Old pieces of sheet music (Figure 8-89) can be mounted with the instruments on the bulletin board.

Calendar

Use 4 × 5-inch cutouts of old music with a solid piece of white paper glued on it to print the calendar on (Figure 8-90).

GOD'S EYES—OJOS DE DIOS

Materials

Ojos made by the residents—see Part V for directions. You will need three to five of the ojos, depending on their size.

To Do Ahead

Have the residents make the ojos.

Directions

1. Mount the ojos on the bulletin board in an arrangement similar to the one shown in the drawing (Figure 8-91).
2. This is a wonderful bulletin board to use with a Mexican theme party.

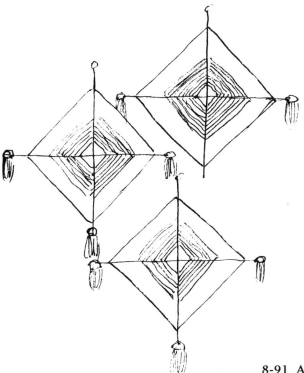

8-91 Arrangement for Bulletin Board

Calendar

Use Mexican hats (Figure 8-92) or Indian basket designs (Figure 8-93) for the calendar. The designs below can be enlarged two or three times for the calendar.

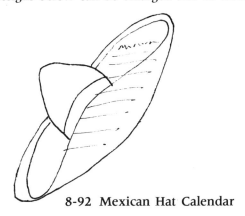

8-92 Mexican Hat Calendar

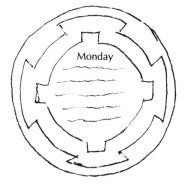

8-93 Indian Basket Calendar

STATE BULLETIN BOARDS

Materials

White poster board, or art paper in colors;
Colored markers;
An outline of your state map or a large and colorful printed map;
Pictures or drawings of your state flower, state bird, state tree, products, or any other identifying items you wish to use to promote your state.

Residents might be encouraged to do research on this board and to decide on the items to display on the board. Any way to involve them is helpful to them and to you.

To Do Ahead

Locate a map in a size needed for your bulletin board. If you are drawing an outline of the state, draw it on the white or colored poster board.

Directions

1. Mount the printed map or the outline cut from the poster board on the bulletin board.
2. Arrange the materials that identify your state on the map in an artistic way.
3. Any designs you need to draw may be cut from the art paper and painted with acrylic paint or colored markers.

Calendar

The calendar can be one of the items used on your state bulletin board. For Texas, we used an enlarged boot (Figure 8-94), but it could have been a hat or outline of the state map.

HOUSES ALONG THE STREET

This is a bulletin board that uses photographs of the residents by placing pictures in each window and several doors. This makes a very interesting bulletin board for the residents and their families.

Materials

Two sheets of white poster board;
Masking tape or tacky glue;
Acrylic paint in pastel colors; pale green, pink, pale blue, yellow, and lavender;
Brushes;
Black marker;
Scissors.

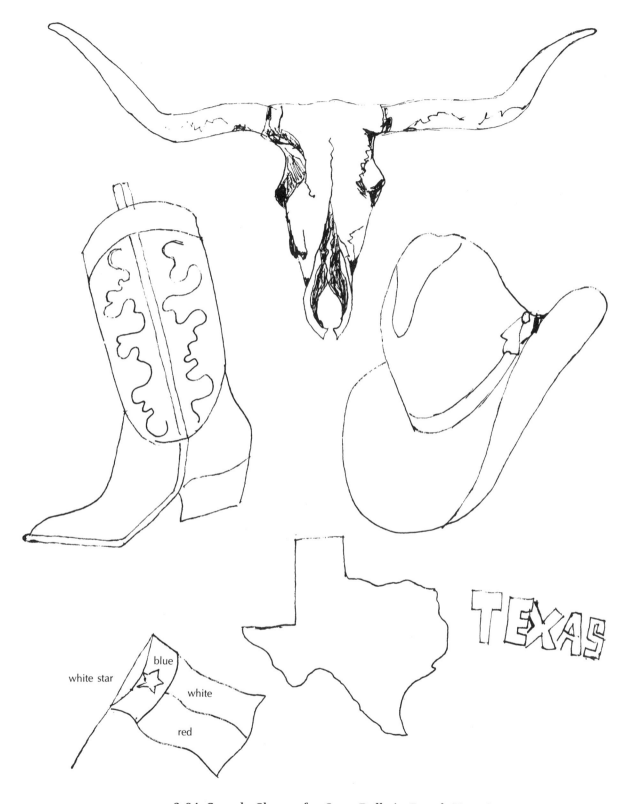

blue

white star

white

red

TEXAS

8-94 Sample Shapes for State Bulletin Board (Texas)

To Do Ahead

Use the pantograph to enlarge the drawing (ratio of 1 inch to 5 inches or a size suitable for your bulletin board). You could also make up your own row of houses if you wish.

Directions

1. Cut the house shapes (Figure 8-95) from the two pieces of white poster board, allowing an extra 1-inch strip for gluing the parts together in the center. Do markings with permanent black marker after painting.
2. Paint the various sections of the houses in the colors indicated on the drawing, leaving the central house white.
3. Cut out pictures of the residents to fit into the windows and doors; glue pictures to the proper place on the house front.
4. Mount the houses on bulletin board.

Calendar

The small cars (Figure 8-96), traced and enlarged three times, with faces glued in the windows, make wonderful activity calendars.

Variations

These houses may be used in October by placing cut-out shocks of corn and cut-out pumpkins beside the doorsteps; it can be used for a Christmas bulletin board by adding wreaths on the doors and small Christmas trees, decorated, along the street. You might even use tiny lights at the roofs' edges or swags of greenery. You can also put stars in the sky. Use your imagination.

LITTLE TRAIN

This is another bulletin board suitable for using with pictures of residents. It would be especially good in summer to indicate travels remembered. Ask questions: "Do you remember the train rides that you took when you were growing up? Tell us about them. Did you eat in a diner or take a lunch? What else do you remember about the train? Where did you go? How far? What did you enjoy most about the train?"

Materials

Two pieces of white poster board to make a train about 35 inches long;
Acrylic paint; black, grey, and red;
Brushes;
Black marker;
Glue;
Scissors;
Residents' photographs

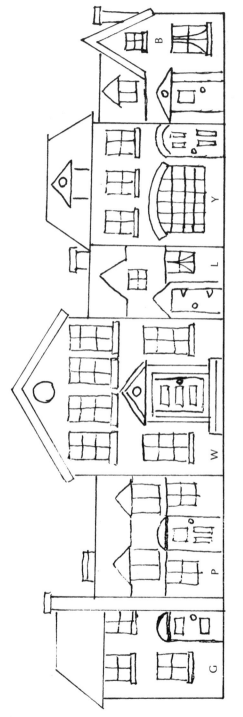

8-95 Houses

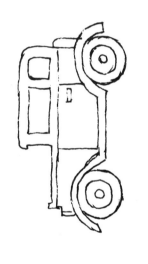

8-96 Car

B = blue

G = green

L = lavender

P = pink

W = white

Y = yellow

To Do Ahead

Enlarge the train to a scale of 1 inch equals 5 inches. This will make a train about 7½ inches high and about 35 inches long. Adjust this size to fit your bulletin board space.

Directions

1. Trace the design on white poster board and cut out.
2. Paint the various parts with the colors indicated in the drawing (Figure 8-97).
3. Cut out the faces of the residents and glue them in all of the windows of the train, including the engineer's cab and the top of the caboose.
4. Mount the train on the bulletin board. You can add extra cars.

Calendar

Enlarge the little suitcase (Figure 8-98) to 3 times its size and use for the activity calendar.

GLOSSARY

Acetate: a material used for cutting stencils; can be clear or slightly milky.

Acrylic clear spray: a lacquer-like clear spray that forms a long-lasting acrylic coating to protect materials.

Batik: the technique of hand-dying fabrics by using a variety of substances as a resist.

Bodkin: a blunt needle-like instrument for drawing tape or cord through a loop or hem.

Calyx: the outermost group of flower parts at the base of the petals, usually green.

Chipboard: a stiff, low grade of cardboard generally made from wastepaper and used as a backing material.

Clay, self-hardening: clay that dries to a hard finish without being fired.

Collage: technique of compiling art by gluing various components on a single surface.

Contact paper: self-adhesive plastic material generally used to protect photographs.

Knead: to move clay from the outside to the center of the mass over and over again, like kneading bread.

Lath: thin, narrow strip of wood.

Motif: a recurring theme or subject, especially in an artistic work.

Mural: a picture painted on a wall.

Pantograph: an instrument of wood or metal used to copy, enlarge, or reduce a drawing on any desired scale.

Shuttle: a device for passing the yarn from one side to the other over and under the warp yarns on a loom.

Slip: a creamy mixture of clay and water used to join and smooth pieces of clay.

Stamen: the pollen-bearing organ in the center of a flower.

Stencil: a design cut out of the surface of an impervious material such as acetate, which, when painted on or inked in the openings, leave a design.

Template: a pattern or mold cut from cardboard or other heavy material which, when used to draw around, forms a design or pattern.

Trivet: heat-resistant object designed to protect surfaces from hot dishes.

Warp: the up and down (or lengthwise) threads of a piece of woven material.

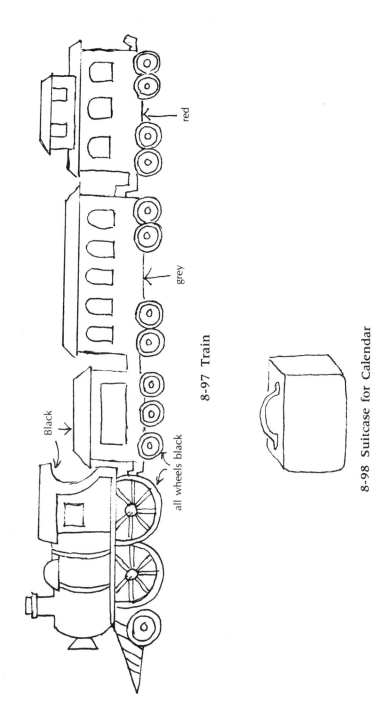

Black

red

grey

all wheels black

8-97 Train

8-98 Suitcase for Calendar

211

Watercolor block: a certain number of sheets of watercolor paper mounted together on a backing from which you tear one sheet at a time; usually comes cheaper than single sheet paper.

Wash: a mixture of paint and water brushed across a piece of watercolor paper.

Weft: the filling (crosswise) threads that are woven in and out of the warp threads on a piece of woven material.

APPENDIX

Many of the craft materials needed for the craft program may be found in local variety stores, craft supply stores, fabric shops, hardware stores, or floral shops. In general, variety stores are the least expensive. To order in quantity or to locate hard-to-find items, check the index of the mail order companies listed below. The first three named can supply most of the materials listed in the projects, but several other companies have been added to assure availability in all sections of the country.

All of these companies will send free catalogues when requested on your facility letterhead.

For all craft supplies:

Economy Handicrafts, Inc.
50-21 69th Street
Woodside, N.Y. 11377

For all craft supplies:

S&S Arts and Crafts
Colchester, CT. 06415

For all art and craft supplies:

Dick Blick Central
P.O. Box 1267
Galesburg, IL 61401

Dick Blick West
P.O. Box 521
Henderson, NV 89015

Dick Blick East
P.O. Box 26
Allentown, PA 18105

Triarco Arts and Crafts
14650 28th Ave. North
Plymouth, MN 55441

For wonderful low-cost books of snowflake patterns, stencils for any subject matter:

Dover Publications, Inc.
31 East 2nd Street
Mineola, N.Y. 11501

For memory-stimulating program material:

Bi-Folkal Productions, Inc.
809 Williamson Street
Madison, WI 53703

For low-cost projector

Norton Products, Dept. D C-3
271 North Avenue
New Rochelle, NY 10801

Materials Needed for the Various Sections of the Book

For Part II—Paper and Papier-Mâché

Various types of scissors;
Ross art paste for papier mâché;
styrofoam shapes;
all kinds of paper from construction paper in sizes up to 24 × 36 inches, to art paper, drawing
    paper, cellophane, crepe paper, tissue paper, foils, and doilies;
acrylic or tempera paint;
crayons;
markers;
nature print paper;
shirt boards;
chipboard;
acetate (25 sheets of 9 × 12 about $4.40);
key chains;
magnet strips;
jewelry findings;
beads;
stencils;
inexpensive brushes and foam brushes;
glues of all kinds.

For Part III—Clay and Clay Dough

Flour;
salt;
oil;
cornstarch;
glues;
clay stamping tools and punches;
acrylic or tempera paint;
paint brushes;
table knives;
rolling pins;
tongue depressors;

paper towels;
and water.
Many items listed above plus self-drying clays including Celluclay, now available in white as well as grey.

For Part IV—Batik

Scissors;
eyedroppers;
vegetable peelers;
objects for rubbing;
glue;
papers;
wax crayons;
string and cord;
clothes pins;
heavy needle and thread;
small plastic;
bobby pins;
balls or marbles.
Dipping paper, cold water dyes, and items listed above.

For Part V—Fabric and Weaving

Scissors;
glues;
trims;
binder cord or twine;
large darning needles;
craft knife;
potpourri mixture or sachet powder;
iron and ironing board;
acrylic paint and paint brushes;
leaves and vegetables for printing;
polyfoam stuffing;
plastic yarn needles;
plastic weaving needles;
simple looms (chipboard looms about $5.00/dozen);
empty yarn cones (about $1.25 a dozen);
burlap and felt;
buttons (in bulk);
ribbons;
yarns;
rug yarn;
and items listed above.

For Part VI—Discarded Materials

Small shells in bulk;
cork coasters;

beads;
sequins;
chipboard;
bird houses and feeders;
wooden toys;
plus items listed above for Part II.

For Part VII—Parties

Throwaways of all kinds;
scissors;
glues;
papers;
acrylic paints;
paint brushes;
markers;
popcorn;
soaps;
yarns;
trims;
old hose;
fabrics;
cork;
balloons in bulk, plus items listed above for Part II.
Many suggestions for each party theme in Part VII.

Part VIII—Bulletin Board Ideas

Papers of all kinds;
crayons;
markers;
acrylic paints;
pantograph or enlarger.

Information on Materials

Clear acrylic spray—a spray-on glaze used as a protective coating to preserve craft work. Be sure to keep the spray holes open and do not spray too thick a coat at one time, but use a light spray several times if needed. This spray should only be used by the director or volunteers and should be sprayed outside or in a very well-ventilated area.

Glue—Clear white glue such as Elmer's may be used on almost any project and will hold most materials. White tacky glue has been used extensively by craftsmen in the last few years. It is clear and flexible and will hold such materials as naturals, fabrics or other hard to hold materials. Spray-on glue is a wonderful, quick, and easy way to apply glitter or anything over a wide area; but it can be toxic, so use only in a well-ventilated area.

Ross art paste or other art pastes are exceptionally good for making papier-mâché paste as they will keep indefinitely without refrigeration. They can be ordered from any of the mail-order houses and are generally available from a good local craft supply house.

Acetate sheets can be ordered very inexpensively from Dick Blick.

Foam brushes are a wonderful choice to use with the handicapped.

Weaving materials such as looms and weaving needles are available from any of the craft supply houses.

Cork rounds are available from S&S Arts and Crafts.

Empty yarn cones are available from Economy Handicrafts.

Papers—Construction paper is probably used by more nursing centers than any other paper and will serve most purposes. It is less expensive, but also tears easily and fades quickly. It is available in sizes 9 × 12, 12 × 18, or from Dick Blick in 24 × 36 sizes.

Art paper is the alternate choice to construction paper. It is a hard-surfaced paper in much brighter colors, is smooth, holds its shape, and resists fading, which can be a great help in some projects where the sun might quickly fade the work. It is more expensive than construction paper, but it's worth it.

Stencils, cut paper snowflake patterns, crocheted snowflake patterns and many other inexpensive pattern books are available from Dover Publications.

Lee Ward is a good source for many of the decorative materials used for making Christmas decorations.

Bi-Folkal Productions can furnish tapes of most of the old music along with other interesting program material. Many of their materials are available on loan from local libraries.

Norton Products show an available "Easy-Copy" projector for enlarging any picture at an unbelievable low price of $19.95 plus $1.95 shipping costs. I have not seen the machine but the advertisement comes through Artists Magazine.

Index